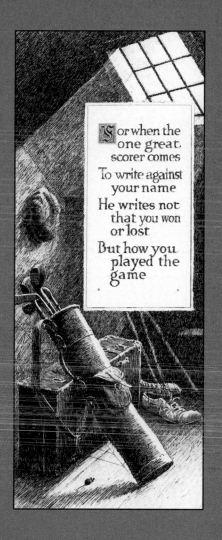

For when the one great scorer comes
To write against your name
He writes not that you won or lost
But how you played the game

Bobby Jones– Stroke of Genius

The Movie and the Man

Forewords by ROBERT TYRE JONES IV,
RICK ELDRIDGE, and JIM VAN EERDEN

Introduction by KIM DAWSON

Text by DAVID SOBEL
Designed by TIMOTHY SHANER

A NEWMARKET PICTORIAL MOVIEBOOK

BRITISH AMERICAN PUBLISHING, LTD.
LATHAM, NEW YORK

Bobby Jones
COLLECTOR'S EDITION SERIES

This publication was initiated and orchestrated by LIFE^{n} PRESS,
in association with Bobby Jones Film, LLC and
the family of Robert Tyre Jones, Jr.

Design and original text © 2004 British American Publishing, Ltd.
Articles, photographs and artwork from *Bobby Jones-Stroke of Genius*
© 2004 by Bobby Jones Film, © 2002 by Robert Tyre Jones IV, Psy. D.

This book is published in the United States of America.

First Edition

Library of Congress Cataloging-in-Publication Data
available upon request.

ISBN 0-945167-54-7

www.britishamericanpublishing.com

A Newmarket Pictorial Moviebook

Produced by Newmarket Productions, a division of
Newmarket Publishing and Communications Company

Esther Margolis, director; Frank DeMaio, production manager; Keith
Hollaman, editor. Text by David Sobel. Designed by Timothy Shaner.

Acknowledgments and Permissions

We are grateful to the publishers and other copyright holders named below for
permission to reprint artwork. Artwork appears on the pages listed.

Courtesy of Bettman/Corbis: 6-7, 110, 118, 123, 128.
Courtesy of Larry Steinbrueck: 15, 66. Courtesy of Sidney L. Matthew: 18
by permission of Emory; 20; 33; 34-35 by permission of Emory; 36
by permission of American Sports Publishing Company; 40; 46
by permission of Times Wide World Photos/NYT Pictures; 52; 58; 63; 66
by permission by William S. Painter; 74-75 by permission of USGA; 78; 82
by permission of Atlanta Journal; 88-89; 95; 101
by permission of Times Wide World Photos/NYT Pictures; 103; 104
by permission of Dundee Courier; 106-107; 109 by permission of Atlanta
Journal; 114; 115; 117; 119; 126-127; 129; 130; 131
by permission of Emory; 132; 149. Courtesy of Jules Alexander/Atlanta
Athletic Club: 86. Courtesy of AP Wide World: 119.
Courtesy of Historic Golf: 142-147.
Courtesy of East Lake Community Foundation: 151, 153.

This book is dedicated to the family of
ROBERT TYRE ("BOBBY") JONES, JR.

*And to all the "Bobby Jones Legacy Partners" who willed this
epic project to life by playing some role in the production,
promotion and philanthropic impact of this film.*

YOU KNOW WHO YOU ARE.

We are ever grateful to you.

BOBBY JONES FILM, LLC
LIFEⁿ PRODUCTIONS

17 March 2004

Contents

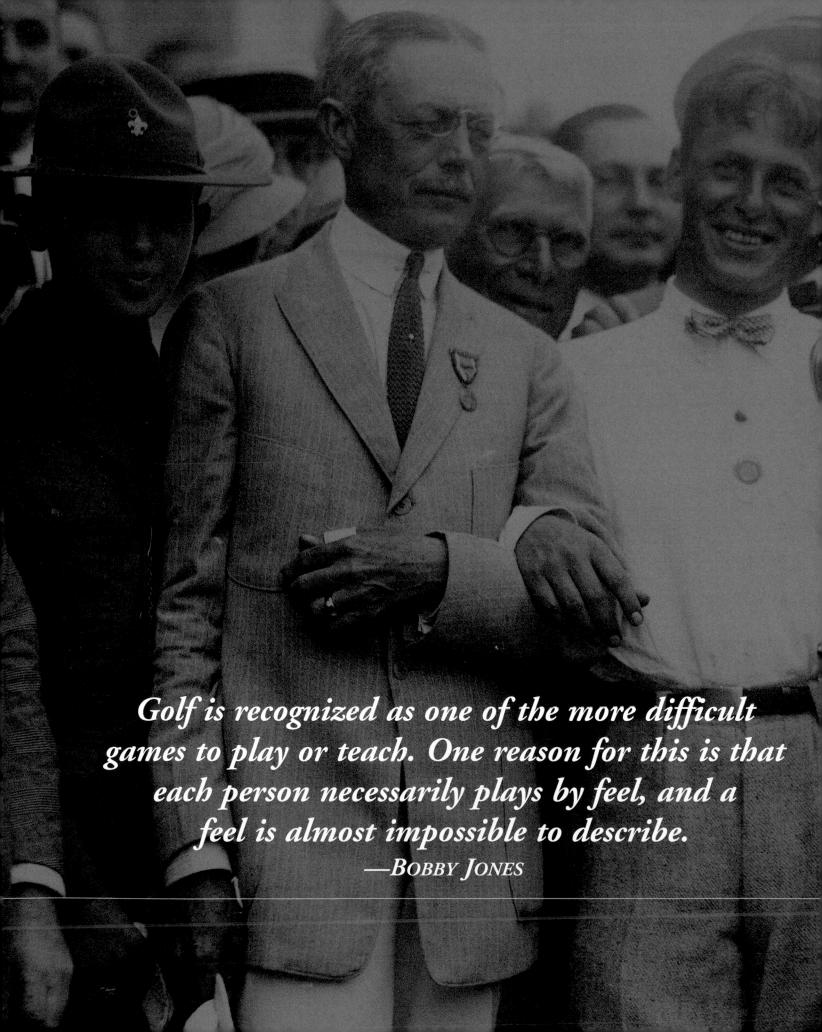

Golf is recognized as one of the more difficult games to play or teach. One reason for this is that each person necessarily plays by feel, and a feel is almost impossible to describe.
—BOBBY JONES

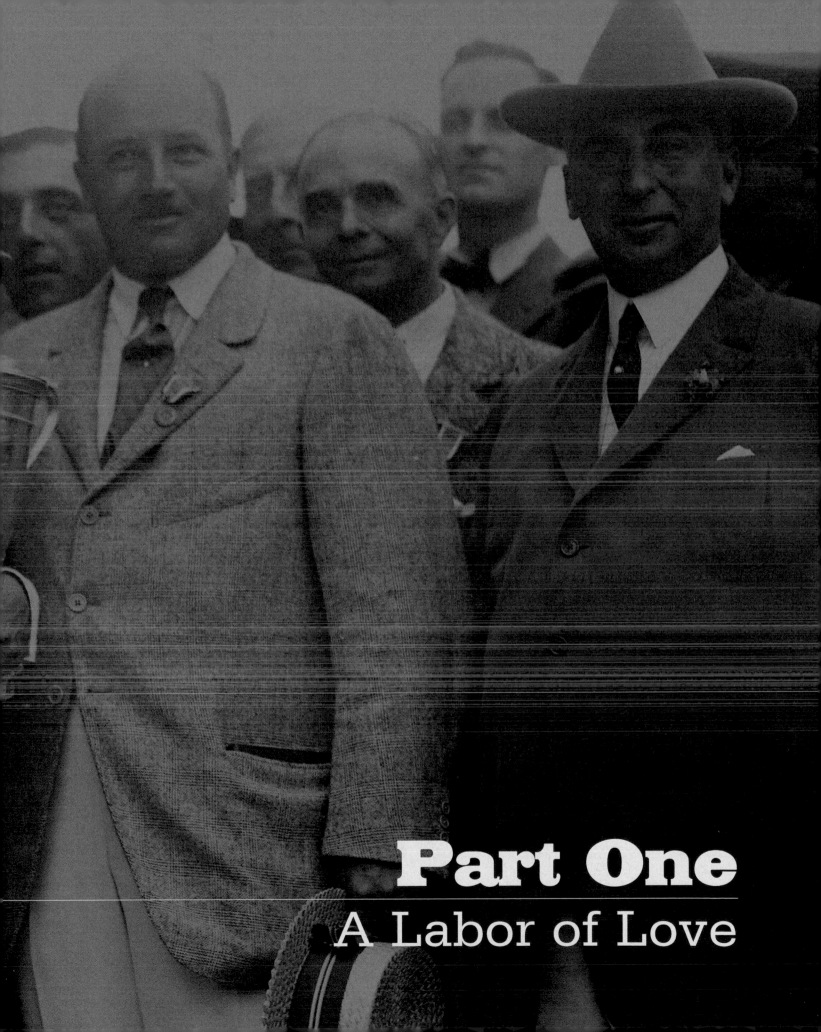

Part One
A Labor of Love

The Legacy of Bobby Jones

by Robert Tyre Jones IV, Psy.D.

How many once-famous people are forgotten 100 years after their birth? Yet more than a century after he came into this world, my grandfather, Robert Tyre ("Bobby") Jones, Jr., is still remembered, admired, and, interestingly, may even enjoy greater popularity than ever. What is it about Bobby Jones that still captures the attention and admiration of the world? Why is he still held up as the ideal champion when other great athletes are remembered only because their name is on a trophy?

I think that one reason my grandfather is still revered is because he was the single most influential man in the history of golf. There is no aspect of the game upon which his shadow does not fall and there is no aspect of the game that he did not alter. I realize that a statement this brash deserves some clarification. Let me elaborate.

First, Bobby Jones lived during an interesting era in American history. He was born in Atlanta in 1902, less than 50 years after the conclusion of the Civil War. When he began to play golf competitively, it was the considered wisdom of the golf world that truly great champions could only come from the northern half of the country. This was accounted for by the fact that most championships were contested on bent-grass greens, whereas southern courses had much slower Bermuda-grass putting surfaces.

I suspect, but cannot prove, that there was also a good bit of regional chauvinism in this statement as well. Bobby Jones' success as a competitor put a quick and ignominious

end to that theory as he won championships on all sorts of surfaces and on several continents. His popularity, both in the North and the South, served as a bridge between two parts of the country that still smarted from the bitter war of the 1860s.

Second, in addition to being a reconciler in his own country, Jones also served as a good will ambassador in the United Kingdom. When he began playing "over there" in 1921, World War I had just ended. Many of us now don't fully appreciate the devastating effect that the Great War had on the British populace. The male populations of entire villages and towns either had fallen on the battlefields of Europe, were severely maimed, or had been rendered insane by their experience. At the time, there were some very bad feelings toward the brash Americans, the "Johnny-come-latelys" who, in British eyes, came in at the end of the war, saw comparatively few casualties, and left claiming that they had secured the victory that had eluded their British allies.

My grandfather came into this potential hothouse and made a phenomenally poor first impression, withdrawing from the British Open at St. Andrews. The British press snubbed him, calling him "a mere boy." But a few years later, when he won his first British Open, he won the hearts of the British and Scottish people—when he asked if the Claret Jug—the trophy given to the winner of the British Open—could remain in Scotland rather than come back to the United States. The ice had been broken between him and the British.

ABOVE: Jim Caviezel with Robert Jones IV, grandson of Bobby Jones.

His relationship with the Scottish people continued to grow and deepen until they took the remarkably unusual step of naming him "Freeman of the City" in 1958. Adding some humor to his touching remarks at that ceremony, Jones said, "Now I can officially feel as much at home here as I have unofficially presumed for years."

In addition to being an ambassador for the game, Bobby Jones changed almost every facet of golf as we know it today. First, he affected the way we currently count major championships. National championships were always important, but did not assume their current significance until my grandfather won all of them in 1930. He set the bar by which all great golfers plan their careers.

Interestingly, when the professionals needed a "grand slam" (since they could not play in the amateur championships), they added the PGA Championship and The Masters tournament. The Masters is the only major that is played on the same course every year, a course that Jones co-designed and a tournament that he founded.

My grandfather effected great changes in the technology of the game. Although he grew up on hickory-shafted clubs, after his retirement he designed the first set of steel-shafted clubs, with wood and iron heads specifically matched to the technology of the shaft. These were as radical to their day as graphite and titanium are to our day, and may even be more so. Why? Simply because in the Robert T. Jones, Jr. clubs the vagaries of hickory were removed: for the first time in history, clubheads were designed to help the average player get the ball in the air. The golfer could focus more on the challenges of the shot and less on the whippy, high-torque shafts of the club and the knife-like blades of the day. This is why the Jones clubs remained the hottest-selling golf clubs for several decades.

Bobby Jones even changed the way we understand the golf swing. His writings are still viewed as outstanding examples of how to describe proper technique. Noted tele-vision commentators have said that Jones' instructional films are state-of-the-art by our standards today, to say nothing of the 1930s when they were filmed. Although top players have developed more efficient and powerful ways to swing a golf club, authorities no less than Byron Nelson and Jack Nicklaus have said that the average player can learn more from studying my grandfather's swing technique than from analyzing the form of any contemporary player. That's high praise from men who are not noted for hyperbole.

In almost every area one can think of in the game of golf, no name holds greater stature than Bobby Jones. The highest award the United States Golf Association gives each year is the Bob Jones Award for sportsmanship and contributions to the game. Scholarship funds in both the United States and Canada have been established in his honor that have raised millions of dollars to support student exchanges between Emory University, Georgia Tech, and St. Andrews University. In Canada, a similar but separate exchange has been created between the University of Western Ontario and St. Andrews University. These exchanges are highly prized within their institutions and the Jones Scholars have gone on to very successful careers.

No discussion of my grandfather's impact on the world of golf, indeed on all sports, would be complete without mentioning his personal code of honor and sportsmanship. During his playing career, Jones conquered a fierce temper and played to a standard of impeccable integrity, several times calling penalties on himself for infractions that no one else witnessed. One time, one of these even cost him a national championship.

When he was disabled by a painful, incurable disease he never complained, but only expressed a determination to "play the ball as it lies." His character shines as brightly today as it did in his heyday, prompting Alistair Cooke to write recently in his book *Memories of the Great and the Good:* "I have done a little digging among friends and old

golfing acquaintances who knew him and among old and new writers who, in other fields, have a sharp nose for the disreputable. But I do believe that a whole team of investigative reporters, working in shifts like coal miners, would find that in all of Jones's life anyone had been able to observe, he nothing common did or mean."

Any one of Bobby Jones' achievements would make for a legendary career. That they are found in one man is remarkable. That they are found in my grandfather is personally humbling. He was, in many ways, one of the greatest men of our era, or any era.

Yet to me and my siblings and cousins, he was just

"Bub"—our nickname for him, coined by his eldest grandson, Bill Black. And memories of the times I was privileged to spend with him, of the advice he gave me and the smiles he bestowed on me, I will treasure all my life. I hope that you will enjoy this book, created to celebrate the feature film, *Bobby Jones—Stroke of Genius*. It is my family's hope that this project will introduce you to the wonderful man who was our grandfather and maybe give you some insight as to why we hold him so close to our hearts more than a century after his birth.

It's About Commitment

by Rick Eldridge, Executive Producer

It has been an emotional roller coaster. A daunting task. First to be faithful to the story and condense what could be, in the words of our writer/director Rowdy Herrington, "a six-hour mini-series." The Jones family has been incredibly supportive and encouraging throughout the process of crafting this story that marks a major part of their heritage and legacy. Golf is just the backdrop—the platform—a God-given gift bestowed on a great man of values, ethics, and honor that should be a model for us all.

An independent film always brings great challenges. The story compelled us to make a film that included a level of production value that pushed the budget envelope for an independent picture. We have been very blessed with a cast we should not be able to afford, an award-winning crew that is tops in its field, and the most beautiful locations one could ever hope to shoot on film. The result is a product worthy of the quality that has always been expected in the name of Robert Tyre Jones, Jr.

This was truly a team effort. Many people from across America have rallied behind the desire to tell this story. It has been a unique three-fold return through financial investment, life experience, and carrying forward the legacy of giving back through our charitable foundation. This commitment of funding by some amazing individuals who caught the vision and supported our efforts in every way has been beyond anything I have experienced before.

Our production team has learned much, grown much,

and endured much. It has been a roller coaster, as most independent film projects tend to be. But we have endured all the challenges. The story is inspirational. The background is golf, but really it's the story of a man who was an exceptional individual with a strong moral character, a keen sense of value in the things that mattered most. It's about his devotion to his wife, his struggles with the hopes and dreams of his father and grandfather, and his fight to overcome his fears and physical limitations. Bobby accomplishes much, yet puts much more value on family and larger life goals. Once he achieves the pinnacle of golf at a very young age, he decides, "I'm done with this. I don't need to be a pro. I'm going to be a husband and do the job that I was called to do." It's a phenomenal story. It's centered around golf because that was a principal part of his life and what he was known for, but the movie allows us to dig deeper and discover the true power and strength of the man.

Everywhere we have been in the U.S. and abroad, people have embraced the Bobby Jones story, just like the people of St. Andrews embraced Bobby as a young man. It has been a phenomenal experience to be involved in the making of such an inspirational story.

This has been a huge undertaking with untold hours of sacrifice by many. I most importantly wish to thank my wife, Krista, and our six children who have endured when I could not be with them and have been totally supportive with their love and concern throughout.

ABOVE: Executive Producer Rick Eldridge in period costume on the Georgia Tech barroom set.

A Story Behind the Story

by Jim Van Eerden, Co-Executive Producer

The effort to finance, produce, and market an independent film is a charming but arduous ambition. In the case of *Bobby Jones—Stroke of Genius*, it required the best of many good men and women, from start to finish, and I doubt that we all would have risen to the task had we not felt *inspired*.

Our inspiration came from this man named Bobby Jones. We sensed from the project's inception that there was a "soul" to it. Indeed, the producers and investors carried a belief that this film was destined to be. Beyond that, we believed that it was destined to be a classic in the stature of the man himself.

This was our mission, and we were all indelibly clear about it. We set out to have our audience respond to our "big-screen Bobby" in a manner not unlike the *Atlanta Journal* editorialist who, following Bobby's historic Grand Slam win, declared: "[Jones] has done more than perform a feat. He has achieved a character, so that the world, while marveling at his game, pays highest tribute to his soul."

This inspiration was a good and necessary thing, as we seemed to have every imaginable obstacle thrown into our path. Inspiration degenerated into sheer perspiration on not a few occasions. Commitments from Hollywood partners to perform, on which it seemed we were entirely dependent, were repeatedly nullified by their non-performance. We sometimes felt as if the movie industry was disingenuous, or simply set against us. Yet we pressed on, believing we had the people, the product, the positioning opportunity, and the business model to make *Stroke* a successful venture.

Of course, in retrospect, we would all admit that our timelines were entirely too ambitious. Our budgets were too small. Our anticipated impact, perhaps a bit too grand. But we set ourselves to the challenge like Henry V's "happy, chosen few," and have been amazed to see so many of our hopeful visions come to life. I have not been part of a work-related team with a stronger sense of destiny and purpose.

So people were willing to work hard. We will all remember Rowdy, our director, literally running to-and-fro between the actors and the camera to save time, so we could complete the day's shots. Rowdy and his crew did this often, exemplifying the heart of everyone we worked with on this epic project. All hands went in. This passion and dedication shows up on the screen.

The film's financing team was led by The Helixx Group, which provides agency planning and implementation services to high-impact entrepreneurs. Helixx develops and refines life stewardship strategies on behalf of its clients, and then creates "SWAT teams" to help them activate their goals. The focus of the firm is to champion what Helixx principals call "Life": an exceptional, unusual, remarkable, outstanding life. Bobby Jones has been referenced by Helixx as one who modeled many elements of Life.

Rick Eldridge, the film's Executive Producer, was the first Helixx client. He introduced the firm to Producer Kim Dawson. Several months later, Tom Crow, Australian Amateur Champion and founder of Cobra Golf, had also become a Helixx client. The life stewardship goals of these three men collided in a wonderful way. All three shared a passion to make this epic film as a part of their personal legacy strategies.

The issue was how to raise the money. We thought it would take us $15 million, then $12 million, then $18.6 million. Chump change for Hollywood. But for us, this

ABOVE: Jim Van Eerden in period costume, in Scotland.

15

was a substantial sum. We wanted to create an epic film, we were told, for "dimes on the dollar." Helixx engaged one of its strategic partners, The Private Consulting Group (PCG), to help get it done. PCG's Managing Directors and their clients came through, and donated the full measure of their enthusiasm to the project. From the heather of Scotland to the decks of the *Queen Mary*, they were there for us with kindred spirits.

PCG is a wealth optimization firm with more than 20 offices across the country, deep client relationships, and unique savvy in structuring private equity instruments, all of which proved vital to the effort. PCG set itself to the task of flipping the Hollywood-film financing model upside down. Traditionally, private equity investors were "first in, last out." PCG and Helixx engaged a guarantor group, represented by Jim Eden, that eliminated the private equity investor risk during the film-production period. Their investment monies would only be drawn down once the film was in a distributable form, and they would be repaid from the property's first net proceeds. In this way, their money was "last in, first out." This approach is quite novel in the realm of film financing.

The other novel element of the Bobby Jones Film LLC investor strategy was our unique approach to return-on-investment (ROI). We told prospective investors that this ROI opportunity would involve three elements of return. First, it would create significant financial rewards. Second, it would generate a philanthropic legacy, involving millions of dollars of donations to charity and millions of people affected by the inspirational message of the Jones story. And, third, the investors' involvement would offer them the experience of a lifetime, through their invited participation in the film-making process, both on and off the set.

There were some mishaps along the way, including a few incidents that threatened to derail us altogether. But we often quipped to one another that "the Good Lord seemed to allow things to go wrong for us so that they could get better." Our match funding partner, for example, default-ed on their match. A major talent agency contracted with us to address the deficit, but did not. A major independent studio then entered an agreement with us, only to themselves default...*after* we had already begun principal photography in Scotland.

But there was a method to this madness, it now seems. In retrospect, people would attach themselves to our project and stimulate us forward, but would not perform. Then another party would advance the ball and do the same. Each time the guarantors, investors and producers stepped up. And on it went until, in the end, we had a great film owned entirely by the amazing people who had, by the grace of God, banded together to will it to life.

So we found ourselves in control of our own destiny. We opted not to forfeit creative, distribution, promotional, and financial oversight to a third-party studio. When we at last agreed this was our course, we were excited. And a bit unnerved. It was a moment of truth. We were a fish swimming upstream, unable to see the river's head, and not absolutely certain that we had the stamina to make the journey. But we were unanimous. With the support of our tenacious investors and each of our families (thank you, my Sweetheart and precious children!), *we all swam hard.*

When everything is said and done, *Bobby Jones— Stroke of Genius* is a success. It is a success because of the spirit in which this epic undertaking has been nurtured and pursued. We have been reminded often of the lines from Grantland Rice that Jones himself held dear:

> *For when the one great Scorer comes to write*
> *against your name, He writes not that you*
> *won or lost...But how you played the game.*

The stakeholders in this project have given our all to play this chapter of our lives well, to point people toward Life^n—those attributes of a well-lived life which Jones demonstrated with such singular grace and distinction. May his legacy of goodwill and integrity continue on through all of us....

Foreword

Following is a list of some of the "Legacy Partners" of Robert Tyre Jones, Jr. Each of them has been a player in "the story behind the story."

COORDINATORS

Kevin B. Atkinson, Joel R. Baker, David M. Breedlove, Jr., Paul & Diane Brooks, Katherine A. Brown, Richard W. Demetriou, Mike Eden, Todd R. Fitzgerald, David J. Fitzpatrick, Bradley E. Graber, Jonathan Greer, David C. Hock, Elizabeth M. & Robert L. Holt, J. Kevin Johnston, Marianela A. Leekley, Michael R. Mathioudakis, David Parks, Carolyn Paul, Kathleen C. Peer, Jim & Linda Priddy, C. Joseph Ramos, G. Matthew Thornett, Richard & Donna Van Eerden, and James & Rachel Van Eerden

GUARANTORS

Tom & Carol Ann Crow, James & Allison Eden, Robert & Nancy Jaycox, Dick & Carol Johnston, and Robert & Lynn Keys

INVESTORS

Mr. & Mrs. Robert W. Anderson, Kevin B. Atkinson, Mr. & Mrs. Virgil R. Barber, Jr., Jeff Barclay, Harriet Barker, James & Tommie Barnes, The Beckwith Family, Rick & Gayle Benson, Nathan & Tammy Birky, Bobby & Laree Black, Larry W. Bonds, Mr. & Mrs. Bontrager, Tom Bosanko, Mike & Kay Breedlove, Christopher P. Brown, G. Scott Brown, Gregory H. Brown, J. Terrell Brown, J. Terrell Brown, Jr., Dr. & Mrs. Bill Burgess, C. Joseph Ramos Family Foundation, Judith & Clifford Cantrell, Dennis Cipcich, Dave & Whitney Colvert, Lloyd & Carol Cox, Bob & Judi Crutchfield, Rick & Louise Demetriou, Denny & Cheryl DiSantis, Kurt A. Dolnier & Allessandra Manning-Dolnier, William & Kathleen Dooley, Mike Duffy, Allison W. Eden, James E. Eden, Michael Eden, Kevin & Valerie Erdman, David, Larlyn, Liam & Fiona Fitzpatrick, Steven & Diane Foley, Johnny & Brenda Folsom, Al & Betty Gladding, Arther & Ruther Glaser, Phillip R. Grace, Jonathan K. Greer, Robert S. Greer, Jr., Charles & Rebekah Gregory, Ray Grimm, Anna & David Grotenhuis, Daniel & Shanna Grotenhuis, Luke V. Guarisco, Dean Bates & Shirl Handly, Joey & Malana Harpst, Jeff Heilbrun, Ann Herrick, Daniel R. Hock, David & Brittney Hock, Rodney L. & Carolyn R. Hock, Robert & Betty Hoerner, Hampton & Nancy Holcomb, Robert & Elizabeth Holt, Bill & Mary Ann Howard, Keith & Jackie Howey, Richard Huber, John & Dorothy Bruehl Trust, Karl & Connie Johnson, Dick Johnston, Kevin & Amy Johnston, Wadene Johnston, Robert L. & Lynn C. Keys, Larry & Nanci King, David & Sandy Kowalski, Robert & Elaine Kuh, Walt & Irene LeFevre, Harvey G. Lowhurst, George & Bonnie Lucas, Stephen & Donna Madinger, Bob Mathioudakis & Family, Mike & JoLee Mathioudakis & Family, Nick & Marilyn Mathioudakis, Bruce A. Matson, Greg & Dara Matters, Stephen & Stacey Mattingly, Bruce & Shari McIntyre, George & Mary Mellon, John & Brooks Moore, John Mouton, George & MaryJane Muller, Clarke A. Nelson, Bill Newton, Cory Newton, Woody Northup & Family, Joyce Oliveto, Gary & Margie Orten, David & Annalisa Parks, James & Barbara Parks, Don & Keturah Paulk, Jim & Diana Paynter, Adam & Crystal Priddy, Jim & Linda Priddy, Joe & Christine Ramos, Patty & John Rickert, Gary & Linda Sanford, Roger & Corey Sanford, Scott & Cassandra Sanford, Stephen & Joyce Schneider Family, Gene & Paula Sherrill, Tim & Kimberly Shrout, Todd & Ann Shutts, Silver Creek Investments, LLC, Rob & Cheryl Sorrell, Mark & Hope Stark, Larry & Denise Steinbrueck, Woodall Taft, Russ & Betsy Taylor, Warner B. Tillman, James & Kathy Watson, Tom & Bonnie Welling, Karl & Lisa Whitten Family, James & Janet Williams, Joe & Dena Wilson, Tom & Mary Wojnas, Milton J. Womack, Arthur & Dianne Wood, North Shore Woods, LLC, Robert F. Zoccola, Sergio & Kim Zorzi

Introduction
How It All Began
by Kim Dawson, Producer

I'd heard about Bob Jones since I was a kid, but mostly only from a golfing perspective. When I first heard that the story was available to be made into a film, I started to learn more about the man he was. I was so impressed by the complexity of the story, and his struggles to achieve what he did, not just in golf, but also in life. It struck me as a story that would, with a great script on a big screen, really capture the hearts of the film-going public. Bob Jones' story has been in the public eye for a long time. People know him as this golf legend who achieved something wonderful in 1930 when he won the Grand Slam, and about his great seven-year run from 1923 to 1930 when he won an amazing number of tournaments. That's common knowledge, but the story is really much more a human drama. I came to understand what made Jones the man he was. He's revered, not only in golf circles, but also in the Atlanta community, in the law community there, and by people who take the idea of family values seriously.

As we started to explore the story, I was fortunate to meet Jane Alexander, a wonderful actress and former head of the National Endowment for the Arts. When she read the script, she told me that the greatest part of this script is that of the friendship between a son and his father, and his grandfather. She felt that the triangle of patriarchs from the South is seldom shown on film, and that theme is one that would resonate with families everywhere. There was a great deal of tension in the family, between Bobby's grandfather, "R.T.," and his father. His father had wanted to be a baseball player when he graduated from college, and was quite skilled at the game, but he was forbidden to play by his father, a stern Southern businessman, who ran the Canton Cotton Mills. The upshot was that Bob's father—"Big Bob" or "the Colonel"—lived vicariously through his son's achievements, and pushed in a way that I suppose was a bit like the way Tiger's dad pushed him into the sport. Knowing that the boy had great talent for the game, Big Bob knew that he also needed to have the support of family and friends to succeed. So, in the end, it's a story of deep family friendship and love—between men and women, to be sure, but especially within that triangle of men. I come from a family of five brothers, and we have a wonderful relationship with my dad, one that in many ways was mirrored by the Jones family. That's one of the themes I wanted to focus on in this story, and I think Rowdy

OPPOSITE: Bobby Jones at the 1927 U.S. Amateur Championship. This was his favorite photograph of himself. ABOVE Producer Kim Dawson, right, with Malcolm McDowell.

19

Herrington, the director, has done that extremely well.

I've been involved with this project for thirteen years. My biggest challenge on this film was perseverance. At some points, doubt creeps into your dreams and starts to infect your belief that something can be as good as you want it to be. Over the years, I've felt that if I didn't maintain a very high standard with regard to the story and how we would present it, I would be doing a disservice to Bobby Jones. I committed early on to the family that we would do it one way only: we would be true to his story, and remain consistent with the truth in spite of having to make an entertaining film and take certain minor license with some historical facts. For instance, we put Jones and Hagen together in a match that never really took place. They were actually on different parts of the course in the 1930 Open at Hoylake, but we had to match them up in order to build the film's drama, and to compress time.

Independent filmmaking is a tough business. You think you have the money and then you don't. You think you've raised the bar up, and then it drops to the floor. You think you have somebody attached, and all of a sudden you find out there's a conflict in their schedule. All of that produces doubt in your mind, and overcoming that doubt has been a great challenge for me. In the end, I have my wife Doreen to thank for keeping me going. Without her undying support I could never have done this. When you have a family and responsibilities, when you've spent literally your whole life savings and a huge amount of time, it's

BELOW: Bob and Mary, right, play a round with Bobby's parents, The Colonel and Clara.

sometimes difficult to carry that around and still keep pushing forward, but I think Jones' own tenacity gave me hope and strength. So did my friend and steadfast attorney Greg Galloway, who wouldn't let me give up.

When I first met Charlie Yates—a legendary amateur golfer, friend of Bobby Jones, and my mentor on this from the beginning—he told me that this would be "like playing a very, very long round of golf on a very difficult course. You have to be extremely patient, and take one shot at a time." I've been fortunate to have Charlie's blessing and support, along with his wife Dorothy and his truly inspirational family.

The Jones family was integral to this project. The heirs had formed a corporation around the estate to protect the name of Bobby Jones. People were trying to draw off the trademark and use his likeness for this and that, so the family needed to act, not so they could exploit the likeness and

name, but so they could protect its integrity. Jones' stature in the game is extremely important to them and to the golfing world. Someone was working on an unauthorized TV film, so I helped negotiate a settlement on behalf of the family and actually consolidated the rights with the help of a business associate, Leonard Witte, who also suggested the title "Stroke of Genius." There is an attorney named Marty Elgison at Alston & Bird, the law firm Jones founded in the 1920s, who became my complete advocate and supporter from day one. I think we were aligned in spirit about our approach to the project. Marty represents all the Jones heirs—seven grandkids spread throughout the United States—and arranged a family meeting with all of them and with Bobby's daughter, Clara, who was still living at that time. They liked the ideas I pitched, and allowed me to go forward and pitch the story to Hollywood studios. Actually, it was a bit of a double-edged sword. I promised to tell the story truthfully and honestly, and not to denigrate the name of Jones. There were some commercial ventures depending on Bobby Jones' good name—the Bobby Jones sportswear line and the Calloway golf club line (Eli Calloway was Bobby's second cousin). But the Hollywood community was completely undone by my promise. Of course, they didn't want anything to do with a movie that required script approvals by a family who didn't know anything about films. Still I felt that the integrity of the man dictated that I behave in the same manner.

Making the Movie

It took me thirteen years to get a script I thought was the right one. I worked on the script myself with writer Tony Depaul, whom I'd known over the years. I really liked his writing style, and his wife had Scottish roots. Together we wrote a script that I thought had great merit. Bill Pryor, a writer from Nashville, Tennessee, lived next door to Jones' granddaughter, Adele. When he heard about the project he wrote another take on the script. Rowdy Herrington, our director, took both versions and rewrote the shooting script. We were extremely lucky to find a director who also brought screenwriting talent to the project. When I met line producer Tim Moore and we started discussing possible directors, I had a very clear vision of how the director should approach this project. I always felt it was a director's film—that it needed the writer and director to be of one mind, and they are on this film because, well, they are the same guy. I interviewed about six directors, but when Rowdy looked me in the

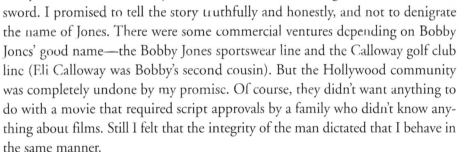

ABOVE: Tom Stern (red hat) and Rowdy Herrington (blue hat) prepare a scene with young Devon Gearhart.

eye and said, "This is not only what I want to do, but I can do it in a way that nobody else would ever do it," I was sold and I've been sold ever since. Rowdy told me early on that he would work harder than anyone else on the set, and when you have a captain of the ship who is willing to work that hard, everybody else just falls in line. He sets an amazing pace, and his work ethic is stunning. He's so well prepared and so caring about every aspect of the film that it wasn't very difficult to get everybody to work as hard as he did.

Casting involved a lot of good fortune. The process began with our search in Hollywood for an actor who could golf. We envisioned that the film would be true not just to the story but to the game of golf, and it was important that whoever played Jones as an adult be able to swing the club the way he did, to be authentic. We searched around Hollywood, and in that process, the script went to Jim Caviezel to play the role of Walter Hagen. When he read it, he said, "I'll do Hagen, but I can do Bobby Jones. I can play this role." We asked him how good his golf game was, and he said, "Don't worry about it. I can play Bobby Jones. I'll get the swing." It was like with Rowdy; when he looked you in the eye and told you he could do it, you knew in your heart he would. So the casting started with Jim Caviezel. He brought a legitimacy to the role that I had envisioned, but I had never expected to get a guy of his stature. He's an amazingly focused and talented actor and a wonderfully warm and kindhearted person. As soon as we met, I knew that the parallel between Jim and Jones was perfect.

We had to make the audience believe that eight-year-old Bobby becomes fourteen-year-old Bobby who becomes the Bob Jones in his late teens and twenties who accomplishes this great feat in golf. We decided to conduct an audition tour around the United States. We went to golf clubs in about ten cities and started looking for a little six-to-eight-year-old Bobby Jones and the fourteen-year-old, as well as some other golfing roles. In Orlando—we started there because that's where I'm from—we found Brett Rice, who plays Big Bob, and Stephanie Sparks, who plays Alexa Stirling. We came up to Atlanta and had an audition at the Charlie Yates Golf Course, right next to East Lake. We saw about 150 people in one day, about half of them were kids. We had laid down the condition that they be able to swing a golf club with some proficiency. We got to about the sixtieth person in the audition, and along comes Thomas Lewis. Our process was that we'd ask a few questions and we were immediately struck with what a warm kid he was. Then he stepped up to the tee and hit the ball, and we were stunned. This kid can flat play the game. He had studied tapes so he knew basically what the

It is often urged that a person playing golf who worries about how to take the club back, how to start it down, and what to do at this stage and that, ultimately loses sight of the only important thing he has to do—to hit the ball.

—BOBBY JONES

BELOW: Rowdy Herrington directs Thomas Lewis on the Bobby Jones Golf Course in Atlanta.

Jones' swing looked like. He could mimic anybody's swing, just like Bobby Jones used to do. For Rowdy, it was love at first sight. Thomas endeared himself to the entire cast and all of the crew members. He's really an engaging young man.

We had about four kids who were primed to play the eight-year-old Bobby, only one of who could actually play golf very well, but we knew that the role had to go to someone with a vulnerable quality. Bob Jones grew up as a sickly kid, and we needed a kid who was less effusive than the fourteen-year-old so that we could show a credible character arc. As soon as Devon Gearhart walked into the room, Rowdy was sold. He said, "Devon will capture your heart," and emphasized that at that age Jones was starting to emerge from his sickliness and beginning to really enjoy life, to live like a normal kid. Rowdy was right on the money. The resemblance between the three actors is just startling, and the personalities are so melded that you really believe they are one.

For Mary Jones, Claire Forlani was on my first list, recommended by my old friend and business mentor Bob Bagley. I was taken by her looks and her charm and her depth of character. But it wasn't until we cast Jim Caviezel that the idea of casting Claire became more realistic. They have the same attorney and it turned out she was available. She's as well-prepared an actor as any I've ever had the pleasure to work with, and she's also a bright light on the set. She brings the same joie de vivre to the role that Jim brings, and you can see it in their rela-

tionship on screen. They have great chemistry, which must be like what Bobby had with his Mary. Clara Jones, their oldest daughter, claimed that there was never a greater love affair. They were like Bogey and Bacall, and it was like that on screen. In real life, Mary claimed that she never kissed another man after she kissed Bobby Jones, because no other man could compare. Even as a devout and conservative Catholic, she was overwhelmed by him, swept off her feet. She didn't know that he was a great golfer, or that he had all these other wonderful traits. He was just the most romantic man she'd ever met.

We cast Aidan Quinn as Harry Vardon. It's ironic that an American is playing the Brit, and a Brit is playing the Yank (Jeremy Northam as Walter Hagen), but it just happened that way. We were about to cast a local British actor when Aidan became available to us through his friendship with our

Introduction

Scottish producer Carol McGregor, and we thought it was
fantastic. He's an avid golfer and has such intensity, such a
presence on the screen, that he really captures his character.
For O.B. Keeler, we needed an actor who had not just intelligence but great experience in acting and in life, and when we
heard that Malcolm McDowell might be available, we knew
that he was the gentleman. Not only does he love the game of
golf in a way that only true golfers do, but he brought humor
and wit to the project that I hadn't expected. The one thing
that isn't that well known about Bob Jones is that he had a
fantastic sense of humor. I think that O.B. Keeler must have
supported that humor and provided a great deal of lightness
to Bobby's life as he went through his struggles on the golf
course. Malcolm just matches that personality so beautifully

that we couldn't have cast it any better. He's perfect for this role. And a wonderful golfer!

Bobby's daughter Clara Jones told me that Bob was great friends with Walter
Hagen, but that his mother Clara didn't really like Walter's influence because he
was such a raconteur. Not only did he love the game of golf, he loved life and
lived it to the fullest. In Jeremy Northam, one of the most accomplished actors
in England, indeed in the world, we found a man who brought not only wry
humor to the role, but also the kind of elegance that Walter possessed. Walter's
approach to golf was that it was a game of recovery. You're going to make your
mistakes, just like you do in life, and if you deal with those mistakes, if you
absorb them and not let yourself be overwhelmed by them, you'll do well.
Jeremy mirrors that sensibility that this is golf, not brain sur-
gery, not war, but that one had a responsibility to the public
and to the game to play with passion and dedication and
respect for history. Walter was a professional, he made a great
living at golf, but he did it with grace and fellowship, and
great generosity. He and Bobby were different in many ways,
but they had that in common. They gave a lot back to the
game, in a great number of ways.

Bobby's mother, Clara, had lost her first child when he
was a baby, and so was very protective of the sickly young
Bobby. She was a cultured woman, with a marvelous mind,
and early on, she taught him literature and the classics. She
taught him about opera, through which he eventually learned
six languages. He would walk down the golf course and hum
arias to himself. He also had a deep-rooted understanding of

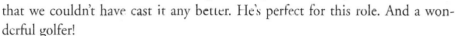

religion and society thanks to his mom. Clara had a great sense of humor and a wonderful sense that life was something more than just what you made it. There was also a divine hand in it, the hand of God. Bobby spoke of his luck and the sense of predestination regarding his life. His mother was also into the occult, which must have set some tongues wagging, but she had a clear vision of what a young man needed in order to be successful in life. With that in mind, she played golf with Big Bob and Bobby at East Lake, and she was not afraid to try anything. I think in Connie Ray, we found someone who captures that spirit. Her joy of life just comes across so well on the screen. You can tell what a caring person she is, and that she doesn't take anything for granted. She's grateful for everything she receives, just the way Clara was, and just the way Bobby Jones was.

Eventually, the cast and crew were set and we were ready to start shooting. Again, we had extraordinary good fortune. St. Andrews in Scotland and its people play such an important part in the story of Bobby's life, and we were the first feature film that's ever been shot on the Old Course. Tom Crow, one of our consulting producers, is a member of the Royal & Ancient Golf Club in St. Andrews, and he had opened the doors for us. Walking onto the Old Course that first day, right in front of the Royal & Ancient clubhouse, was a humbling experience. St. Andrews is the home of golf. Everyone who plays the game seriously wants to make a pilgrimage to St. Andrews, to establish that they've really played the game the way it was meant to be played. It's hallowed ground. The R&A is the home of the rules of golf. Even the USGA picks up its rules from them. It is one of the most prestigious places in the world of golf and to be able to shoot on their grounds and have access to their clubhouse in a way that nobody else ever has was amazing. And it was the association with Bobby Jones that made it possible. He is so revered in the city of St. Andrews. It was Bobby, in a sense, who opened the doors that we wouldn't have been able to open otherwise.

Lifting Our Hearts

When I started this project, I imagined what people might say as they were leaving the movie theater, and the one that keeps coming back to me is, "I'm glad I saw that, because it lifted my heart." Bobby Jones had a special spirit. Everything about him gives you the feeling that there is hope for us human beings, that there's a reason to live that's more than just winning a golf tournament or doing well in court, or whatever. His advice, in golf and in life, was to do the best you could—give it your best effort and be proud of that effort. (The same effort given me all along the way by my Mother, who passed on during this project.) In the end, you'll find that if you've done that, you can hold your head high. You can walk through the world and smile. I believe that people who learn this story will have the sense of Bobby Jones that I have, and leave the theater enriched with that same feeling.

OPPOSITE: Although this portrait by William Steene was painted from a photograph, the details, such as Bobby's clothes and his grip, were taken from real life.

Bob was a fine man to be partnered with in a tournament.... He made you feel that you were playing with a friend, and you were.
—GENE SARAZEN

Part Two
Re-creating History

Number 224
50c.

SPALDING'S
ATHLETIC LIBRARY

HOW TO PLAY GOLF

"HOW I PLAY GOLF
by BOBBY JONES

A REPRODUCTION OF THE TEXT AS SPOKEN IN THE BOBBY JONES SERIES OF GOLF INSTRUCTION

Produced by Warner Bros. Pictures, Inc.
and released by the Vitaphone Corp.

Elation and Fear

by Rowdy Herrington, Director and Co-writer

My first reaction when I heard about the project was both elation and fear. Elated because it's really an amazing opportunity to dramatize a man's life that was as rich in character and complex as Bobby Jones. Fearful in that I knew that this is a story that's likely to be told only once, and it had to be done well. That's quite a responsibility, and I took it personally. Bobby Jones was such an exemplary character, and lived his life so well that I felt a real responsibility to do the best I could to make his story come to life on the screen.

One of the things I like to tell the crew is that enthusiasm is contagious and I don't think you're going to find a producer with more enthusiasm for a subject than Kim Dawson has for Bobby Jones. That set the tone. It was clear from the beginning how passionate he was about this project, and how careful he intended to be in the selection of the people who were going to work to realize his vision.

I worked with Kim and Rick Eldridge to implement structural changes to the original script, changes that would make the story work. It had been framed initially as a story that took place primarily in 1930 during the Grand Slam. I thought that might not be the best way to show the development of the character of Bobby Jones. By that time, Bobby was already a champion, and in many ways fully formed. I thought it was important to see the changes in his character—the "arc," as they say. To see him go from child to adult and then to see him go from adult to leader and then to see him go from leader to visionary—that was a clear and meaningful progression.

I've always been a writer/director. For me, writing is the primary art. It's the most creative act. It's where things come out of the heavens, so to speak. You create something from nothing. You take something that is essentially blank and unformed, and give it life. Directing, on the other hand, is more interpretive. It's a little easier in that you already have the framework. Also, you have a lot of people to help you. Writing is solitary, but I happen to really enjoy it. Directing is an opportunity to collaborate with very talented people, and that is a great deal of fun. It's a lot more fun to direct than to write, I can tell you that. Writing is

ABOVE: Rowdy Herrington behind the camera. PRECEDING SPREAD: A jubilant crowd hoists a triumphant Jones after his first U.S. Open victory. OPPOSITE: The cover of an instructional book culled from Bobby's short films.

harder. They are two very different processes, but they come together in one sense: both writers and directors are storytellers.

I was attracted to this project because it is a bona fide drama. I've been working in genres for a long time. Hollywood is very fond of action/adventure and suspense, for instance, and I've made my living doing that. This is my first opportunity to make a movie where there are no guns. Nobody walks into a room and pulls out a gun and starts telling everybody what's going to happen. This relies on character, on honest human emotions and motivations. We watch these people in a crucible, where things happen to them; forces act on them and they change and they make decisions that illuminate what life is really about for all of us.

But there was so much more drawing me to this film. It's been a dream come true, not only because I'm a golfer and a golf fan, but because Bobby Jones is such a phenomenal character, and because we've had the opportunity to go to a lot of places that most people never get to see up close. I went to the Old Course in St. Andrews, East Lake in Atlanta, Brookhaven, and Augusta National to name just a few. We filmed on all these courses, places that had never allowed a feature film crew before, and it was thrilling. It really speaks, not to me or to our producers or to the great crew we had, but to the one person who gained us entrée into all these places: Bobby Jones.

Just as golf is a game of recovery, so is life, and that's the theme that runs through this movie. Things happen. You have setbacks and roadblocks. No matter how prepared you are or how lucky you get, things don't always go your way. You have to move on, and do the very best you can.

—ROWDY HERRINGTON

The Jones family encouraged and supported me. Bobby was a very good man. There wasn't a lot of controversy swirling around his life. It's not like we were doing the Larry Flynt story, or some other character about whom different factions felt differently, and over whom there had been a great deal of argument. Here was a guy who was simply good, and naturally the family was concerned about how he would be portrayed. That's their legacy to protect. They read the script, and we had a great meeting that left me feeling very confident. We got to one point where they were concerned about a scene in which Bobby has something of a breakdown. But I explained that I took that scene from Jones' own account in his book *Down the Fairway*. I spoke about how a crisis like that occurs when someone gets so emotionally locked that they can't go forward, and Jones' grandson, Bob Jones IV looked at me and said, "My grandfather was a very emotional man," and that was the end of the conversation. They signed off on the script and

we shot exactly what I wrote, and now the audience will decide.

I had wonderful people working with me on this movie. We had a cinematographer named Tom Stern who had just come off *Mystic River*. He's as smart a guy as I've met in the film business, and delightful. When you see the film, you'll see how beautiful it looks, and that's Tom. I was also very lucky to get my friend Bruce Miller to be the production designer. Bruce and I had worked together a couple of times before, and it's wonderful when you can work with people with whom you have a long-term relationship. Bruce is phenomenally talented, and what he was able to accomplish on the small budget we had is spectacular. I couldn't have made this picture without my spectacular first assistant director, Richard Graves. In Scotland, we had as many as 350 extras, and more who weren't recruited. We had 250 in Atlanta, and to dress all of these people and get them on the set and organize them in the number of shooting days we had was a staggering challenge. The amazing Beverly Safier did the costuming. Another place where budget could have held us back was on the music, but I fought to get the right composer. I knew this was a small independent film but it deserved a big score, and I was thrilled when James Horner not only became available, but was so taken by the film that he wanted to participate. I just had great people all around me. That's what it takes. They worked like dogs, and they should be very proud.

Golf is a game of recovery, as they say, and when you're making an independent film, and you don't have the kind of schedule and budget that studios provide, you have to be lucky and you have to be prepared. I think we were both. We were very fortunate with the weather, and miraculously lucky with the people who signed on for this film. We went out every day and did the very best we could. My father told me long ago, "Do your best, sleep well at night." We have done our best, and only hope that people respond to our work. Just as golf is a game of recovery, so is life, and that's the theme that runs through this movie. Things happen. You have setbacks and roadblocks. No matter how prepared you are or how lucky you get, things don't always go your way. You have to move on, and do the very best you can. I think Bobby Jones is the personification of that idea. I hope that people see Bobby's life in a way that has meaning for them. I hope that we were able to bring the film together with life and truth and honesty and with the power that it deserves.

OPPOSITE: Shooting the 1918 War Relief matches scene with Jim Caviezel and Stephanie Sparks as Alexa Stirling. ABOVE: Cinematographer Tom Stern at work.

Jim Caviezel
On Playing Bobby Jones

ABOVE: Bobby pitches out of the "Cottage Bunker" at St. Andrews during the 1930 British Amateur.

I knew very little about Bobby Jones. I just loved the story, and I felt that (despite having just played Jesus) I couldn't think of a finer man to play. I read the script and saw how the other characters saw him, and what he said and how he lived. That's what attracted me. I did my own investigating, and talked to a lot of people, including Bobby's granddaughter, and asking what they thought of him, how they remembered him.

But no man is perfect. We tend to forget all the other things that maybe he wasn't so great at. Like his temper. But in order for a piece of coal to change into a diamond, it has to undergo some serious heat and pressure. I just kept thinking, here's a guy with three degrees. He's a lawyer, and an engineer, and he knows English literature. Being so smart, being an engineer, and trying to hit a golf ball must have been so frustrating at times. I kept imagining Bobby thinking, "OK, I did all the math, so why is this ball going way over there? Why did I slice it?" I thought about that, about utilizing that frustration, and it made it easy for me to throw a golf club.

When you play someone like the Count of Monte Cristo, nobody ever says, "Well he walked this way or he looked like this or he fenced this way." And then with Jesus, people might not know quite the way he walked or sounded, but everybody has some idea about it. But when you play Bobby Jones, everybody in Georgia know how he talked, walked, ate, spat, drank. So I think that made it pretty hard.

Then there was the golf swing. There's nothing I hate more than watching a basketball movie, because I used to play in college, and spot immediately a guy who doesn't really play. Maybe he addresses the free-throw line wrong or his elbow is out or something, but I can just tell if he doesn't have the knack. I did not play much golf before this. I hit it around a little, but I just substituted what I knew about shooting a basketball for hitting a golf ball. The one thing that all athletics have in common is balance. As soon as I found my center and balance, it was much easier to learn. I think we got it about 95 percent there but I wanted

to make sure that any professional golfers who saw this film could slow the stroke down and believe that I had it.

But I think it would be a shame if people were to think that this movie isn't for them because they aren't into golf. This film transcends golf. It's about a human being with an extraordinary amount of integrity, something money can't buy. Any time you have an ailment as a young person and you have to overcome it, it gives you an edge. You have to work harder at things, and that work ethic pays off later in life. You find that people like that tend to want to excel. They can't settle for being average. They have to step up and do things better than that. I use that in my own life, for example in sports. I had to work for it. And acting was the same way. Maybe my work ethic is how I compensate when things didn't come easy.

It's a great film for young people who are trying to find their way. Nowadays, sports stars and other celebrities say, "I'm not your kid's role model." It's an excuse to act however they want, to make huge amounts of money. But Bobby wasn't about that. He was a guy who embraced the idea, who said, "Yes, I am a role model. I'll take that responsibility." His pureness drew me to him. That's my own heart, and exactly the kind of characters I like to follow and at least try to emulate.

I kept imagining Bobby thinking, "OK, I did all the math so why is this ball going way over there? Why did I slice it?" I thought about that, about utilizing that frustration, and it made it easy for me to throw a golf club.

—JIM CAVIEZEL

Claire Forlani
On Playing Mary Jones

Mary Malone met Bobby and became Mary Jones, his wife and the mother of his children. There was actually very little written about her, but her grandson, who knew an incredible amount about her, had gone into depth with the producers of the film. I really think the script captured her essence. She was a devout Catholic and there's a beautiful true story about her. Later on in life, when Bobby Jones was in a wheelchair, he was on the second floor and a fire started in the house and she couldn't get him down. So she just sat next to him, prepared to die with him. It showed who she was, and their love, and I feel that's definitely the story we're making. It is so much a story about golf, but I actually said yes to the role because Rowdy and Jim really felt this relationship was such an important part of who he was, that it would explain the decisions and choices that he made.

Bobby and Mary both said they fell in love at first sight, but Mary's parents were Catholic and Bobby wasn't, so I think there was a big religion issue. But he converted before he died, for Mary. There's a great line in the script about Mary dealing with her parents. Mary's father asks her if Bobby is Catholic, and she replies that he is not. She's been dreading this because she knew her father was going to be pretty hard-core about it. Then the father asks, "Well, what have I told you about that?" And Mary turns around and says, "You told me judge not, lest ye be judged." I thought that was a perfect line.

Later, O.B. Keeler and Mary are kind of caretakers. They're the support, the backbone of the family. They're the ones that watch Bobby, and know him and understand him. O.B. and Mary trade off going through Bobby's emotional journey. They try to help him and balance him and be there for him and watch over him, because he's somebody who is all or nothing. You've got to stand by people like that.

When you speak to golfers, they say that Mary was the one who made Bobby quit golf. Whenever there's a female attached to a man in sport people think it's the Yoko Ono–John Lennon syndrome. Mary wasn't trying to stop him from playing golf. I don't think two people could love each other that much and try to control each other. For me, it was about her understanding and her love for him, knowing that he was killing himself and it wasn't bringing him happiness anymore. It was about the pain she felt watching him suffer for everyone else.

Later on in life, when Bobby Jones was in a wheelchair, he was on the second floor and a fire started in the house and she couldn't get him down. So she just sat next to him, prepared to die with him. It showed who she was, and their love, and I feel that's definitely the story we're making.

—CLAIRE FORLANI

Bobby and Mary

In *Stroke of Genius*, Bobby sees Mary sitting in a coffee shop and is instantly smitten, so much so that he chases her down the street into a trolley. Although Jones may have been struck by such a thunderbolt of love in real life, their meeting was somewhat less cinematic. Mary Malone came from a middle-class, third-generation Irish-Catholic family in Atlanta. Not only was she in high school with Jones, but also knew him through her brothers, who, like Bobby, were very involved in sports, through which they had all become friendly. There's nothing fictional, however, about the deep and abiding love between Mary and Bobby that's depicted in the film. Their relationship is remembered by friends and family alike as one of the great and true love affairs that lasted undiminished throughout their marriage.

ABOVE: Mary and Bobby, 1923.

Malcolm McDowell
On Playing O.B. Keeler

.B. is like everybody's favorite uncle, and uncles never change. They're always kind of the same, and then they're kind of gone. In this story, Bobby Jones starts out as a young kid and goes through until he retires from the game of golf at 28, so of course he changes, but O.B. just stays the same. In a way, Bobby's impression of O.B. would be one of timelessness, and I think that's a good choice. I'm there to play his mentor, somebody that Bobby can trust. He's the man that Bobby always trusts, even—especially—when things aren't going well. He's "O.B. Wan Kenobi." He's the master.

O.B. first saw Bobby when he was a fourteen-year-old boy, and I think O.B. realized that here was a very special young man with a rare and amazing God-given talent. Bobby Jones was not an easy man to get to know. He was rather stoic. O.B. had to earn Bobby's trust, and he did it with his love for the game and with his writing. And they spent so much time together, with all the long travel in those days. I feel bad for the Colonel, Bobby's father. He had a law practice and had to earn money to send Bobby all over the country and to Europe to play in these championships. He couldn't always accompany his son, and in a way, O.B. became a father figure, but if the Colonel was half the man I think he was, he would have been grateful that somebody was there to emotionally support his son through difficult times.

Even though there's a huge age difference, I think O.B. really saw what an extraordinary human being Bobby Jones was. He loved Bobby, but I think honestly that O.B. was generous enough to know that the only thing that really mattered to him in the end was Bobby's happiness. And I think he was thrilled when Bobby found a partner, and had a family and all that. O.B. even admired that Bobby gave everything up.

When you meet great sports personalities or great actors, as I've done, you know there is something about them that is different. I don't know what it is; maybe a sort of charisma. But I think it's actually a belief in the self that is so inherent that it's never questioned. It's like predestination. A lot of great sportsmen have this—they know they are going to win. When they are defeated, as everyone eventually is, it's so psychologically shocking. Muhammad Ali had it. He came back and won again and again. It's why people like Ali and Bobby Jones are so special. It's just something else. It transcends the sport.

I was writing baseball but thinking most about golf, which was just then beginning to emerge from the chrysalis, you might say, as a game to be written about. Talk about luck. There was a kid named Perry Adair, and a younger one, named Little Bobby Jones, beginning to be talked about, in a golfing way; and a little redheaded girl named Alexa Stirling at East Lake, was precisely three years before winning the first of three national championships.

—O.B. KEELER, FROM *THE BOBBY JONES STORY*, PREFACE TO THE 1953 EDITION

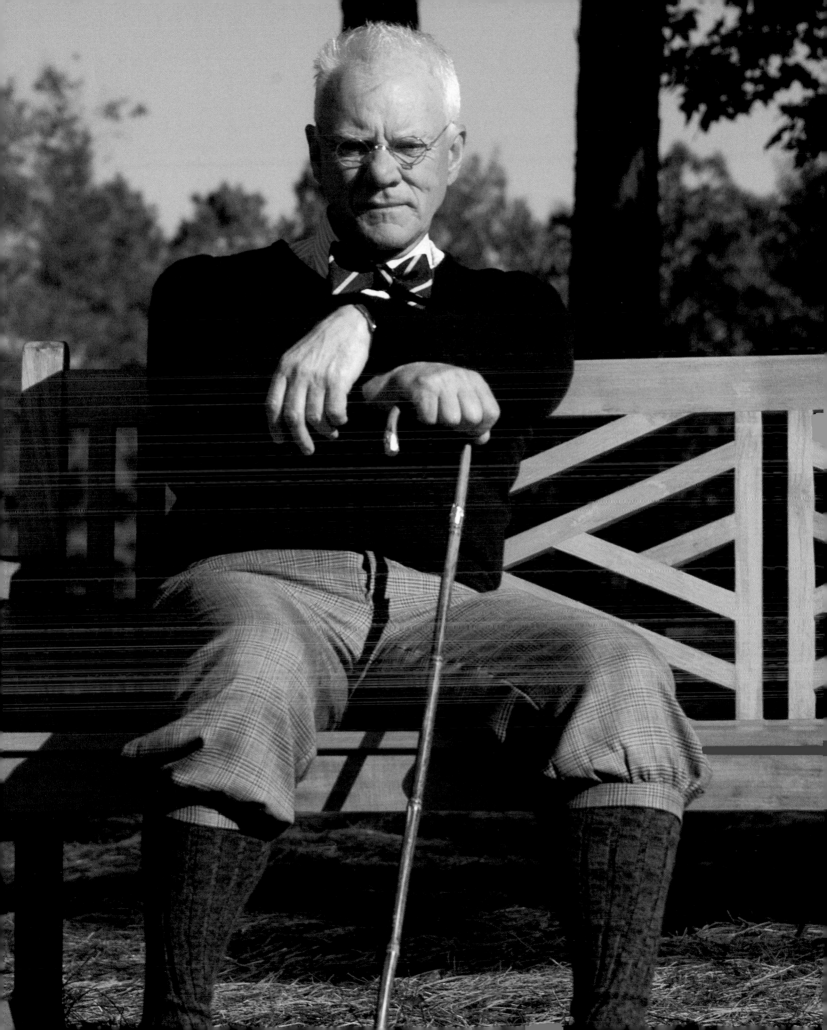

The Real O.B. Keeler

Few sports writers have ever been linked so clearly and directly with one of their subjects, as Oscar Bane Keeler was with Bobby Jones. Not even the much-discussed relationship between Muhammad Ali and Howard Cosell rivals the closeness of Keeler and Jones. Keeler was born in 1882, and grew up in Marietta, Georgia. He was a newspaper man inside and out, a top-quality writer and reporter who, along with Grantland Rice and others, set the standard in the field during the first half of the twentieth century. He was already an established and respected writer and authority on golf for the Atlanta Journal when he first met Bobby Jones at the Georgia State Amateur Tournament. Bobby was only fourteen at the time, and the Georgia Amateur was his first significant tournament win, but Keeler was captivated by the boy, and by his potential. From that moment on, Keeler made it his primary business to cover Jones' career. Over time, the two became the closest of friends, with Bobby turning to Keeler for advice about both golf and life at critical times. Amazingly, O.B. was on hand for all of Bobby's major championships. He logged roughly 150,000 miles of travel with Bobby, chronicling just about every stroke the young man played in competition. Later, O.B. wrote the definitive biography of Jones, still in print today, and helped Bobby write some of his own books on golf.

Keeler wrote in a style that was characteristic of the time, somewhat overwrought and occasionally melodramatic, and with a bit less objectivity than is expected of journalists today. He might make a passing mild reference to a possible shortcoming or to some less-than-stellar play, but he was generally unabashed about his admiration for Bobby Jones. "The gods of golf used all they had to keep Bobby from winning," he wrote after Jones' first U.S. Open victory. "Three times they managed it, and it had also taken a miracle round at Skokie to bar the door the year before. This time Bobby stood up under a smash of fate that would have sent a weaker man into the discard, and he met the gods of golf at their own game and defeated them. I shall never feel that it was Bobby Cruikshank that Bobby beat in that last round. It was fate itself. And it takes more than a great golfer to do that."

It might seem as if it was a rather one-sided relationship, with Keeler's own professional success so dependent on Bobby's meteoric rise to the pantheon of golfing greats. But Bobby, always thoughtful and humble, knew that he needed Keeler as much as, if not more so than, Keeler needed him. "If fame can be said to attach to one because of his proficiency in the inconsequential performance of striking a golf ball," Bobby said, "what measure of it I have enjoyed has been due in large part to Keeler and his gifted typewriter."

As much as Keeler's chronicle helped immortalize the Jones legend, his support and encouragement made it possible. The scene in which O.B. takes Bobby aside just before a match and exhorts him to believe in himself holds more than a grain of truth. Keeler described it later: "At last he had the idea. At last he had begun to realize the power of his own game, to believe what I had tried to tell him at St. Louis in 1921: 'Bobby, you will win championships just as soon as you come to believe that when you step out on the first tee with any golfer in the world, you are better than he is.'"

Brett Rice

On Playing Big Bob

Bobby Jones' father played a huge part in young Bobby's life. When Big Bob started playing golf, he would take the boy out on the course with him, just to walk along. It not only helped establish a relationship between father and son, it really improved the boy's health. And, I believe little Bob would watch his father play golf—badly sometimes, I might add—and see him slamming clubs on the ground and using words we don't normally use in polite company, and I think he picked up not only his temperament, but his sense of humor and at least the beginnings of his values from his father.

The most important research I did was with O.B. Keeler's book, finding out about the relationship between O.B. and Big Bob, and how it related to little Bob. Big Bob and O.B. became friends and confidants to each other. Bob went to O.B., and said, "Would you help my son? He respects you, and his temper is getting the best of him. He's not winning tournaments because of this. Maybe you could talk to him. It would be a personal favor to me." You don't find that kind of camaraderie, that kind of friendship nowadays. It's very rare to let another gentleman help your own child over a hurdle that you can't help him with yourself. You have to swallow your pride and ask for help.

Big Bob's own father was not interested in his son playing games. I think that letting little Bobby follow him around on the golf course was one of the reasons Big Bob and his son became such good friends. It could be that Bob is living vicariously through Bobby Jr., through his playing golf and succeeding in the way Bob thought he could have succeeded in baseball, but we have to be careful presenting that. We don't know if he's spitting back in his father's face, or if he's trying to show his father that this can be done, that people can grow into decent human beings while playing a "frivolous" game like golf or baseball. That's what I was trying to find out in my research.

I was attracted to the role because even though Bob lived as his father had told him, he gave his own son the opportunity to follow his own heart, and be happy. I was attracted by the love he shows for his son. It's not spite he shows for his father, but he actually tries to educate him with the idea that you don't have to follow in someone's footsteps to be a good human being, to make a niche for yourself in the world and to support your family. If you follow your heart and follow your dreams, and do it sincerely, then you've got everything.

Connie Ray
On Playing Clara Jones

The script described me as slender and tough as steel wire. I don't think you have to act abrasively in order to be tough. You can be kind and understanding and gentle and still be as hard as a rock, and I think that's exactly the way Clara was. The great thing about playing Clara Jones is that you go from 1908 to 1936. This is a huge time span and it's at a time in American history when women are in such flux, in the midst of such great change. The suffragette movement happened when Clara Jones was an adult and a mom, and all of that had to influence her, with the education she had, and what she could instill in her son. What a great role to play. It's also great that Clara gets to play golf. In 1908, they lived beside a golf course, and she doesn't stay home and make the cookies and serve the tea when the men come back from the course. She's on the course, out there swinging with everyone else. Excellent.

As a mother, she was overly protective, but she'd already lost one baby, which broke her heart, and little Bobby was sick, wouldn't eat, and was close to death. She wasn't willing to have her heart broken again. She was the mama lioness protecting her cubs. She'd do anything to keep her baby alive, and once he was thriving, to see him succeed. And he was a spectacular kid who grew up to be a spectacular adult. The investment paid off. I don't think Big Bob and Clara disagree about how to raise Bobby. We come at it from different directions, but we have the same goal in mind. We expected great things from him because he was capable of such greatness. I don't think you can be great without obstacles to overcome, and Bobby did that in a spectacular way. And we helped him as parents.

If Clara had a problem with someone, it was with Walter Hagen. She thought he was a dangerous man. He was a great supporter of Bobby, and certainly helped him and became his friend. But Walter represented the outside world, and some of the bad things about golf. Golf was hard on Bobby, and it gave him so much strife and pain, in addition to the success.

Devon Gearhart
On Playing Bobby Jones

I play the part of Bobby Jones. *Little* Bobby Jones. When he was little up to when he was five years old he was very skinny and frail. And he used to want to play baseball all the time, but his mom would say, "No, you can't play baseball because you don't weigh enough." And he fell in love with golf when he was six years old. He had a very hot temper.

In my own life, I'm like Bobby. We kind of look alike, and we are both perfectionists. Another reason why I'm like him is that both started loving golf at an early age. We both are very athletic, and we love golf. And reading.

My favorite part of making this movie was getting to play golf. I got to learn the Bobby Jones swing. To do the stance and everything took me a couple of weeks. I had to hit the ball towards the crew, and it was like a pinball game. I had to hit this big square silver thing, but then I'd hit a camera, or I'd hit someone in the head, and they'd ask me to do it again. Also, I had scenes with the puppy, Judge. I would give him treats so he would follow me everywhere, and it was really hard because I had to do my own acting and then I had to help him do his part.

My favorite scene is where I get to start playing golf, except for I don't like the word I have to say. Golfing and acting—it's pretty cool. Bobby Jones likes his dog, he's smart, he loves to play golf, and he has a horrible temper. That's basically what he's all about. He expects a lot from himself, and this is what, over time, helps him to be so great at golf and so good in life.

ABOVE: In his earliest known golfing photo, six-year-old Bobby takes a swing at East Lake.

Thomas Lewis
On Playing Bobby Jones

ABOVE: Fourteen-year-old Bobby at the U.S. Amateur Championship 1916, at the Merion Country Club.

When this role came along, it was a little closer to me than other things I'd auditioned for. This is Bobby Jones. It's golf. Golf is my second passion and I just love playing, and I had studied Bobby Jones all my life. I've done tons of reports on him. I went to audition the first time, and they asked me what I knew about Bobby Jones. I just started talking about how Bobby was the only player to win the Grand Slam—all the majors, the ultimate in golf—and how he did this and did that and graduated from Georgia Tech, and they were just amazed. I wanted it so bad and I tried my hardest. I went on about six auditions and finally they called and said, "You got the part."

It helps if you play golf for this part because you have to know the background. Bobby had a very different kind of swing. He would knee-hitch it. And back then, the swing was a lot different anyway, had a different finish. I met up with Chad Parker at East Lake who had studied him. He took a look at my swing and told me I chase after the ball, which is one of the things that Bobby Jones did. Chad told me I was unique because not many people when they come up will have fast hands and chase after the ball. I had to learn the way he would come up to the ball and bring his knee in. I had to learn his chip, his putt, and teeing off. But it was fun.

I like O.B.'s relationship with Bobby when he was my age. He was just amazed at this kid. The friendship was just starting, but O.B. really admired that Bobby played for the pure love of the game, and that he just went out there and played to win. I think Malcolm McDowell fits that role. There couldn't have been a better person to cast for this, because Malcolm understands the relationship so well, and we react to each other the same way. We really had a vibe. He's not only a good actor, he's a really good friend and such a great person.

If I could talk to Bobby Jones today, I would tell him that this is not just a movie about him. It's a movie about the game. It's a game of skill, a game of tradition and grace and finesse and there are so many ways you can do it. The game is just amazing, and Bobby Jones played for the fun, for the good times, not for money and fame and all that. He loved the game for the game. Today you don't really find that. When I step onto a golf course, I cherish every moment of it.

A Visual Concept

by Tom Stern, Director of Photography

What interests me most about cinematography is the telling of a story. I find that the better understanding I have for a story, the better I am able to come up with a visual concept. The period of 1910 through 1930 is extremely lush. It's a time of profound transitions—there's an industrial transition going on, a fashion transition, a transition from a horse-drawn world to a mechanized one. The whole pace of life accelerated about ten fold in those twenty years. There's a cultural and historical element, as well as a mise en scene—solitary players against these verdant, pasture-like backgrounds—both of which attracted me.

I don't like to establish a period feel through diffusion. Rowdy and I decided early on that a wide-screen format would be ideal for this film. I used Super-35 and was able to create a fluidity and an ultimate sharpness with lyrical lenses. I think we succeeded in re-creating the period without any filters. I didn't want to create some kind of artifact that felt distant from the viewer. I wanted the viewers to be able to suspend their disbelief, to forget the world of 2004 for an hour or two and feel like they were right there, living and empathizing with these characters in 1920 or 1930. We used the Steadicam a lot which helped us get all kinds of shots. We were able to move fast and take advantage of crowds or other spontaneous happenings. We had great camera operators who were able to pick up stuff in crowds or do background while we were focused on tight shots or other specific things. Generally, we were very fortunate with our crew, with the weather, with locations, with everything.

This was a challenging film, with time constraints and budget constraints. We had to go like hell, of course, but in the midst of all that chaos, I wanted to create an island of tranquility around the camera, so that the actors never felt rushed, and so that Rowdy would have the proper space to work with them and respect their craft. Having a great crew was part of what made that possible. So was good planning. If you do a lot of planning, you make your own luck. I knew what I had to do, and had it all laid out neatly so that we could refine it or change it on the fly when we had to. You have to plan well to give yourself the room to change quickly. That's what lets you take advantage of magical little moments of serendipity, like when an actor really sinks into a part, or an accident of nature or availability occurs. It's what the great Conrad Hall used to call serendipity.

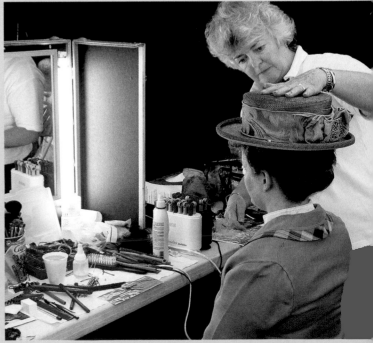

Thread by Thread
by Beverly Safier, Costume Designer

A lot of Bobby Jones' life is on film and in pictures, but I worked more generally from the period—the cut, the look, how the clothes hang. We had to have a lot of fabrics made for us that would look right, and would have the right properties of the costumes in the pictures and the newsreels. The first time I met Rowdy Herrington, I said, "I want to create Bobby Jones thread by thread." And that's what we did. Over the period of the shoot, we changed approximately 35,000 costumes, which is a much larger number than I ever set out to do. But to keep the clothes looking fresh and different, we had to change the wardrobe daily. And of course, we had to jump between periods. Bobby Jones had 82 costume changes ranging from 1908 to the 1930s. O.B. Keeler had 37 costume changes and Walter Hagen had about 17, but his had to be special. Each costume had to say something about the man.

I loved working with Claire. She wore everything beautifully and made the costumes look great. She was really the only one on the set who I worked with on a one-to-one basis. We had to be very careful with her dresses, the cut and style. Her frame is so so slight that a lot of color could overpower her. A lot of print could overpower her. We had to go very simple and plain.

Overall, we kept a muted palette, and stayed with as many earth tones as possible. That was keeping with the colors that were appropriate for the period. We used a lot of herringbones, windowpane plaids, and a lot of tweeds. Those were the fabrics that were primarily used in the era we were shooting.

One of the luckiest things was that Pringle in Scotland came on board and helped re-create all of Bobby's sweaters. They opened their archives and copied their 1920's sweaters for me. They closed their factory and did only our work to help get Bobby Jones wardrobe ready. They did his socks! Bobby Jones would never have looked so good without their help. And they didn't charge a penny—one of the oldest knitwear companies in the world. I think it was because of their desire to see argyles come back. It's truly an amazing story.

ABOVE: Beverly Safier's drawings for Mary and Bobby Jones with argyle socks. BELOW: James Priddy, an investor, in costume at the St. Andrews shoot. Photo courtesy of Linda Priddy.

Music on the Wind–James Horner

There were a lot of people who felt because *Bobby Jones—Stroke of Genius* was an independent film with a limited budget that the producers and director had to be realistic about who they wanted to compose the music for the film. But they all had in mind one man—James Horner, the Academy Award-winner and 2003 nominee for his score for *House of Sand and Fog*.

"When I was thinking about the music for *Bobby Jones—Stroke of Genius*," said producer Kim Dawson, "I kept coming back to James Horner's haunting, emotive film scores such as the theme from *Titanic*—a soundtrack that is alive and memorable—almost like another character in the film."

As luck would have it, James Horner was not working and had an open time slot. He agreed to come and see the film. "This was one of the highlights of this production for me," said director Rowdy Herrington. "He was so taken by what he saw and told us that he was very interested in doing this movie. I know this is an independent film but it deserves a big score so we all agreed to talk and try to figure out a way to accomplish that."

"One of the things that attracted me to this project," said Horner, "is the legendary nature of who Bobby Jones was and the beautiful way this was expressed in this film. Jones' story was one of extraordinary skill, talent, and accomplishment that was matched by great humility and courage. In *Bobby Jones—Stroke of Genius*," continued the composer, "Rowdy Herrington has made an exquisite film that provides a wonderful canvas for music and I'm so thrilled and honored to have been asked to compose the score."

"The addition of Horner completed the incredible team of gifted talent which we were so very fortunate to secure," agreed Dawson. "We believe Mr. Horner's music will provide a powerful emotional undercurrent to the stunning images captured by our director of photography Tom Stern and the strong performances which our director Rowdy Herrington elicited from an amazing cast."

ABOVE: Composer James Horner
RIGHT: Michael Andrews singing
"Almost Famous."

What the Camera Feels
by Bruce Miller, Production Designer

This era, the first part of the twentieth century, was very interesting to me. We had a limited shooting schedule and limited budget, and I knew the challenge of getting the period details right under those guidelines. We could have spent another six months researching, but the problem is that you can spend all that time, then find a photograph, if you're lucky, of what Bobby's house looked like, for example, and it could be completely inappropriate for the movie. It might say the wrong thing about the family. They didn't decorate to please modern audiences, so we might have to create the right look. We used one house that was actually a county museum, but some of the furniture would make the family look wealthier than was appropriate. We wanted to show them as basically normal people.

Often, we wouldn't have time to move the production, so I would have to have four or five or even six different sets at the same locations somehow, so that we could just go from one to the other. That works best for the golf scenes because you can just turn around and face a different direction, as long as you're conscious of little things, like the type of trees or the denseness of the foliage. But sometimes the background just blends into green, and we could make liberal use of close-ups. One golf course could be used to represent many.

We had a lot of luck. For instance, Bob and Mary lived in a neighborhood where we were shooting. It was a house that we found driving down a street while we were out on a scout. We noticed the house because it had copper gutters, or what we now know are fake copper gutters. But these are the kinds of things that dictate a lot of choices that you make. We found a lot of locations—offices, houses, hotels—that looked like the period. Some even were connected to Bobby Jones somehow, because he left little pieces of himself all over Atlanta. We'd just have to be careful about things like telephone poles and the wrong kinds of windows or wall switches or driveways, and anything that might give the place away as being too modern.

We also lucked out with hiring of the production company in Scotland.

ABOVE: The young Bobby Jones accepts a trophy. BELOW: Concept watercolor by Andrew Duncan of the Capital City Club at Brookhaven.

They just kind of arrived in St. Andrews, and once I told them what to do, they just ran with it. And of course, St. Andrews is simply, well, St. Andrews. American golf courses look totally different from European ones, especially the older ones, especially the classic links courses. The hard part was turning the camera around so you weren't looking at the North Sea.

Our biggest challenge was probably doing that little town-square scene when they arrive in the car. It was only about the third day of shooting, and we could only dress the scene the evening before. The town council helped a lot. They sent two guys who, with a plan of St. Andrews, took down light poles and street signs and anything else you don't want there. I wish American cities would do that. Even with that kind of help, we had so little time that it was hard to make this scene as big as it needed to be.

You never know exactly what the camera will see, or "feel." You just hope. And I think things turned out really, really well.

ABOVE and BELOW: Scenes from the movie filmed in St. Andrews, Scotland.

Everything That Had Wheels

by J.L. Parker, Transportation Captain

Sometimes when I see a movie it really bothers me to see a car that wasn't even made yet in the year shown in the film. So I'm real true when it comes to not getting something that's newer than it's supposed to be. And I try to get an original car that hasn't been souped up or modified from the way it was originally.

For *Bobby Jones—Stroke of Genius* I used more than 40 cars. Three were for Walter Hagen. Big Bob Jones' car in the film is a 1908 Buick, which we felt was close to what he actually would have driven.

As transportation captain I was responsible for everything that moved on wheels associated with the film. That included all the trailers used for wardrobe and makeup. This film required the biggest wardrobe trailers we could get and then we had to bring in a couple more for storage!

My wife, Cindy, is the transportation coordinator and she does all the planning and budgeting. I work with the teamsters because I'm a local teamster captain and this was a union film.

All of the cars for *Stroke of Genius* had to be earlier than 1930. The earliest is 1902. To find the cars, I went to museums, car clubs, and private owners, and arranged for their use. When the script is calling for a car that's almost 100 years old, you're not going to run down to the local car dealer for that!

Some of the vehicles in the film were horse-drawn, like the sickle that was used to mow the greens on the golf courses. We were only able to track down three of those sickles in the whole country.

After close to 30 years in the movie business, I've worked on a lot of films. I knew about Bobby Jones before the film, but I learned a lot more. I was honored to be chosen to work on this project.

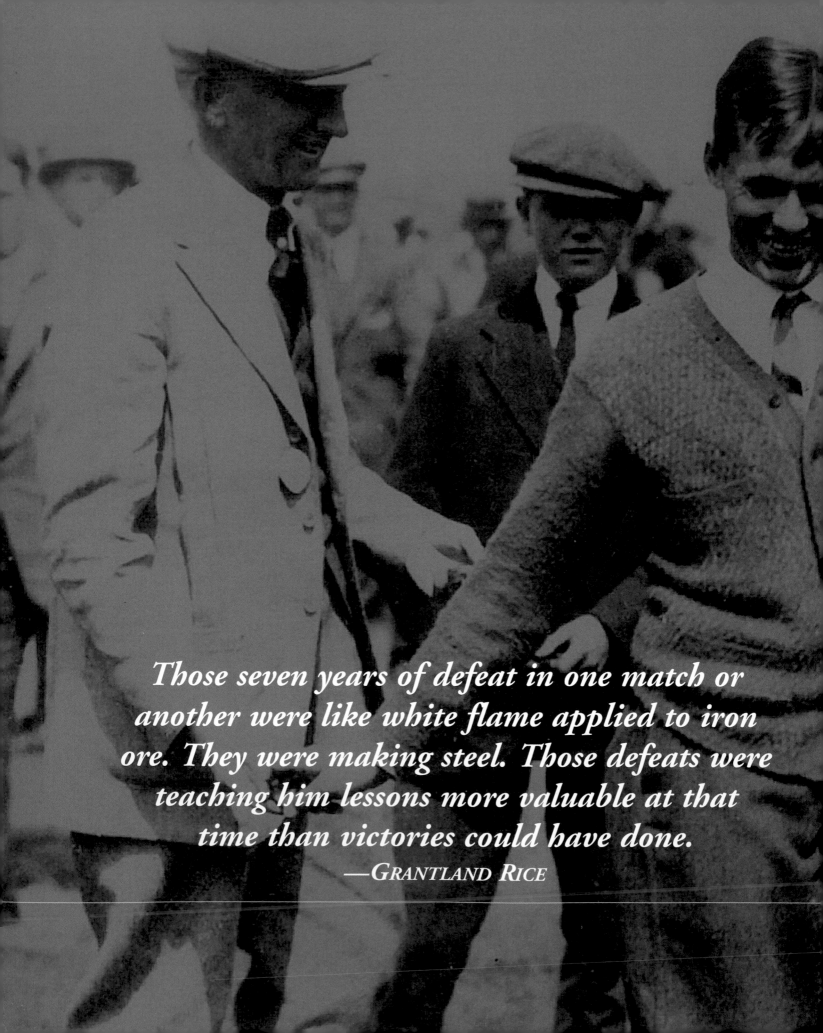

Those seven years of defeat in one match or another were like white flame applied to iron ore. They were making steel. Those defeats were teaching him lessons more valuable at that time than victories could have done.
—GRANTLAND RICE

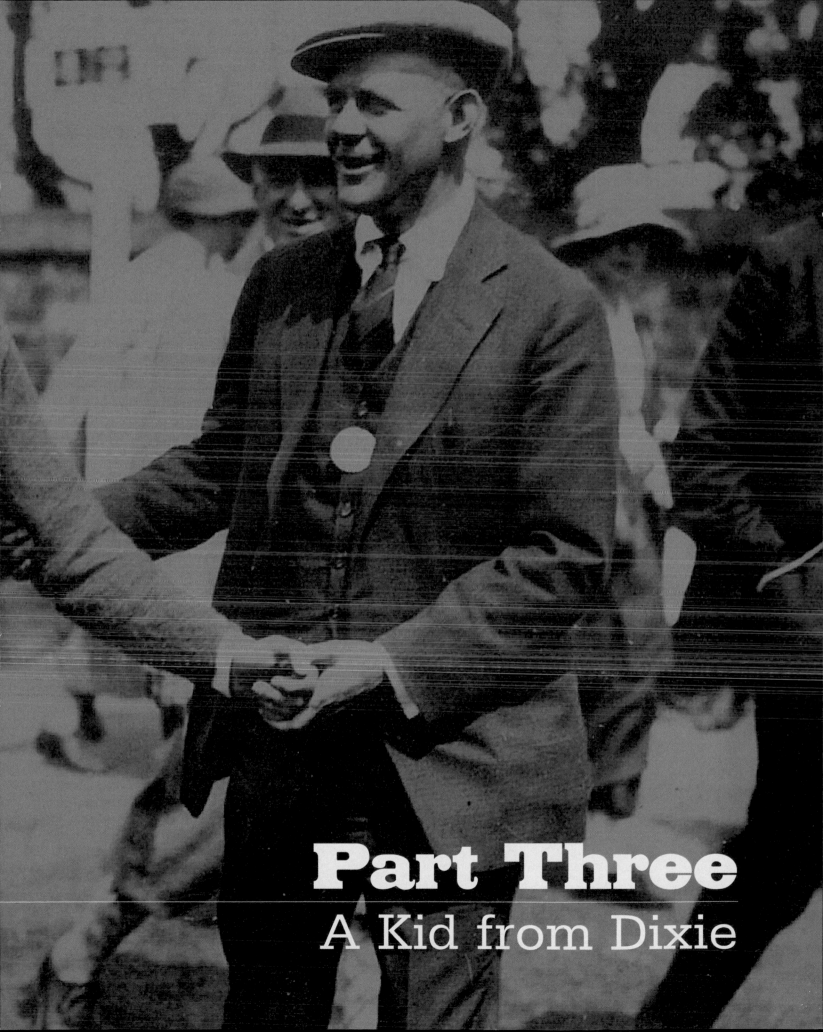

Part Three

A Kid from Dixie

1902-1916

When Colonel Robert Purmedus Jones of Atlanta and his wife, Clara, welcomed a new baby boy into the world on March 17, 1902, they chose to name him after his paternal grandfather, Robert Tyre Jones of Canton, Georgia, yet they appended a "Jr." to his name anyway. Grandfather Jones was a force to be reckoned with. The owner of the Canton Cotton Mills was, for all intents and purposes, the lord of Canton, Georgia, and presided over the affairs of that small mill town like a man born to power. He was revered, having kept the company and the town healthy and solvent during the times of war and economic downturn. "R.T.," as he was called, was a stern and pious man, set in his ways—the old ways, but little did the old man think that the birth of this boy would permanently alter his world view, and in some ways help usher in the modern age for the Jones family.

The third Robert Jones in as many generations came to be called Bobby, thus making it necessary to call his father "Big Bob." Big Bob, like his father before him and his son later, was a man with a great force of will and a powerful independent streak. As a young man he had been a very promising baseball player, but had reluctantly, perhaps even bitterly, given in to his father's insistence that he abandon such a frivolous pursuit. (Later, the elder Jones was equally displeased with his grandson's attention to golf.) Nonetheless, Big Bob chose a profession that suited him—the law—rather than join his father in the family business. He built a respected practice in Atlanta, and established a full and rewarding life for his young family there. It wasn't until he and Clara felt a pressing need to provide more outdoor space for their sickly young son that they moved out to the suburb of East Lake and joined the golf club there.

Little Bobby was indeed a frail child, pale and underweight. Bobby barely ate solid food before age five, and was so weak and slow to develop that his parents quite literally feared that he would not survive. Having lost one son already, Bob and Clara were not willing to take another risk, and removed the child to the warmth and open space outside the city.

Stewart Maiden

By all accounts, Stewart Maiden was just as he is portrayed on screen (by Scotsman Alistair Begg). He was a compact man, but somewhat intimidating because of his dour manner and stern visage. Maiden came from Carnoustie, a place well known to golfing fans, and the sultry American south was something quite different from his gray and blustery Scottish home. It was Maiden who first recognized Bobby's natural talent, and encouraged him, giving him his first set of handmade clubs, and letting him tag along with adults on the course. It is said that Jones never took any formal golf lessons, but Stewart Maiden knew Bobby's game inside and out, and kept a helpful eye on him throughout his playing career.

Bobby's delicate health is likely responsible not only for his developing a love of golf, but also his love of books and reading. His parents discouraged him from sports and other strenuous exertions. From the earliest age, Clara read to him constantly and later made sure he always had some book in his hands, and not just some children's fluff, but even from the earliest age she had him reading works of lasting literary significance. But Clara didn't create a scholar out of her son. The boy was possessed of a keen, incisive intelligence, a prodigious memory and curiosity, and was blessed with a mother who fed his insatiable hunger for knowledge and intellectual challenge. Throughout his childhood, Bobby applied himself as intensely to learning and schooling as he did to golf, striving for perfection in all things, while always maintaining his own perspective on the relative importance of sports in the greater scheme of life. Bobby Jones still stands as the ultimate embodiment of the "scholar-athlete."

Bobby's obsession with golf was sparked at a young age, and developed quickly. Young Bobby couldn't join the neighborhood boys in their baseball games, but he could certainly watch the grown-ups across the road hitting their golf balls and he could tag along with his parents on their weekly round. He started out with a single sawed-off cleek (a one-iron) which he and another boy used on their homemade course in the yard. Despite his lack of size and strength, Bobby was a naturally gifted and graceful athlete, able to master correct and efficient form simply by watching others. He was lucky to be able to model his golf swing after that of the East Lake club's pro, the Scotsman Stewart Maiden, who had recently arrived in America to take over the job that had belonged to his brother Jimmy. Maiden had a classic swing that Bobby was able to mimic with ease. He also mastered the less perfect swings of his parents' friends and golfing partners at East Lake, and would amuse them all with his antics. Indeed, Bobby would tag along with his parents as they played their rounds, and on his own he would scamper through the woods shadowing Stewart Maiden and the other golfers, always watching, always learning. It was Stewart who finally gave the boy a workable set of clubs, cut-down clubs he had carefully fashioned himself in the East Lake pro shop.

Bobby's good childhood friends included, as the movie suggests, Perry Adair, three years his senior and a very strong competitive golfer in his own right, and the lovely Alexa Stirling, who also lived on the East Lake course. Alexa went on to become a national champion herself, winning the U.S. Women's Amateur Championship in 1916 when she was barely eighteen. She won that tournament twice more in 1919 and 1920, and numerous other titles as well. Alexa did indeed beat little Bobby at a tournament for kids organized at East Lake,

First Win a Loss

Bobby's first trophy was indeed a modest little cup he got for winning a children's tournament organized at East Lake. It is commonly believed that Alexa Stirling properly won the tournament, but that club officials were reluctant to give the trophy to a girl. Golf historians are fond of describing Alexa as the only girl ever to beat Bobby Jones in formal competition. Although Bobby did try to do the right thing and turn the prize over to Alexa, he ultimately accepted the little cup, and treasured it in a way that only children can.

Rogers Fell Before Perry And Thrasher

Nashville's "No-Hit" King Is Outpitched by Atlanta's Bear-Cat and "Watkinsville Walloper" Finished Him With a Mighty Home Run

DOUBLE - HEADER DIVIDED

After Crackers Had Beaten Rogers in First Game the Vols Captured the Second Behind Air-Tight Pitching of Dick Wells

BY MORGAN BLAKE

THE great arm of Scott Perry and the mighty bat of Frank Thrasher proved too much for the illustrious Tom Rogers, pride of the Nashville hurling corps yesterday and the "No-Hit" King bit the dust in a grueling pitching duel to the tune of 2 to 1. The Vols however came back and won the second contest of the double header by a similar score. The haughty league leaders left our midst last night and they were mighty glad to depart. They managed to win two games of the five and they were darn lucky to get them.

Both games yesterday were highly exciting and nip and tuck from first to last. The initial engagement early developed into a pitcher's battle between Perry and Rogers and Scotty far outshone his rival in the box. For six innings not a hit was made off the delivery of the Cracker bear-cat and when Atlanta made one run in the sixth it looked like Scotty had a shut out battle at least as the contest was only scheduled for seven innings. But Dick Kauffman singled to start the seventh, went to third on two infield outs and scored on Gabby Street's timely bingle to center.

This necessitated an extra inning and after Nashville had been retired in the eighth Frank Thrasher backed the game away. Two were out at the time and nobody on when big Frank stepped up to the plate. The fans had settled down for a long extra inning game when Rogers shot over a ball to liking of the Watkinsville walloper. Frank swung on it with all his force and lifted it over the right field sign. He trotted around the bases while the tremendous crowd in the grand stand and bleacher raised a mighty din. Frank got an ovation and also something a little more substantial in the nature of a fat purse from the audience.

IN this game Scott Perry continued the wonderful work in the box that he has given vent too in the past month. In the third inning he walked three men and filled the bases, but retired the side without a run. Up to the seventh, as stated above, not a hit was made by Nashville. Two hits in the seventh counted a run and two hits in the eighth threatened but did no damage.

Atlanta's first run came in when Yerkes singled and stole second and scored on Mayer's single to left. This was in the sixth inning.

In the second game the Crackers were helpless before Dick Wells, who held them to three hits and one run. This run was scored in the first inning when Tex McDonald led off with a triple over Lee's head and scored on Reilly's sacrifice fly to left.

Nashville's two runs came in the second when Kauffman singled and scored on Roy Ellam's long drive over Mayer's head for three bags. Roy tallied on Marshall's slashing single to left.

After this round, Ad Brennan pitched a game holding the Vols to one hit in the remaining five innings. But the damage had been done and with Wells pitching airtight ball the Crackers could not retrieve. In the second Mayer singled, went to third on Munch's hit to center and was caught at the plate when he and Munch tried a double steal. This was a mighty close play and to many it looked like Sammy had beat the throw. But Umpo Moran ruled different and his word was law.

FIRST GAME

CRACKERS	AB.	R.	H.	O.	A.	E.
McDonald, 3b						
Reilly, ss						
Moran, lf						
Thrasher, rf						
Yerkes, 2b						
Mayer, cf						
Munch, 1b						
Perkins, c						
Perry, p						
Totals						

VOLS	AB.	R.	H.	O.	A.	E.
Lee, cf						
Sheehan, 3b						
Baker, rf						
Williams, lf						
Kauffman, 1b						
Street, c						
Ellam, ss						
Gilbert, 2b						
Rogers, p						
Totals						

Score by innings:
Atlanta ...
Nashville ...

SECOND GAME

ATLANTA	AB	R	H	PO	A	E
McDonald, 3b						

Young Bob Jones Who Captured Final Match in State Golf Title Tournament

Great Sport Carnival Here on Labor Day

Held Under Auspices of Atlanta Federation of Labor—Randolph Rose Will Stage Big Boxing Contests, Bringing to Atlanta Some of the Most Prominent Pugilists in Country. Other Events Will Be Foot Races, Baseball Games, Etc. A Great Gala Day

ATLANTA'S greatest athletic carnival, the like of which has never been staged here before, is on the card for Labor day, starting in the afternoon and running into the night.

last Thursday President R. M. Gans placed Mr. Rose on the amusement committee, and he was at once elected vice chairman of this board.

Acting in conjunction with W. C.

YOU reach the Brookhaven a across the wa brassie shot over the and a long iron to long hole and a hal a long fight and a ha on the eighteenth h Little Boy Jones won championship from P

It was almost toiling over the la after a day of gruell each youngster had p of his career. A was trailing them, and women restless heribly hot.

They had watched on the last eighteen hole match with Per rival. They had seen lead to two up at th had watched him, pla that he hardly hear hole until he had on Number eleven an up on sixteen. Th the next hole and no Little Bob only one test.

TWO long drive the center, two the crest of boys took their irons win on the green, bo from the cup. Perry edge where he could he could do the w and hole out in one p the match and have on the nineteenth hol

But it was too m man, much less a ni who for hours had nerve and muscle a most sickening silen thing on one little hole until he had on His putt was tw hole. Bob's putt s a six. Perry took the match was over

AS the youngste center of the a patter of a the crowd. And wi ing a champion, the well for the vangu all for an exhibitio that has not been do links since Scotland As a finish to t tament ever held Jones-Adair match be desired in the w put up by the two the quantity of cri hairraising thrills step of the way.

Both boys played lives. They drove approaches were per they ran down puttin

The figures on the speak for themselve a 70, Perry a 75, par and came back par.

I HAVE never se life," said a v the match. "w Vardon, Evans and I I don't believe any have beaten Bob Jon going on that last was weird, somethin the realms of huma came supernatural. thousand and did in ways he proud that saw Bob Jones and their famous encoun

The gallery that will agree with him gallery that ever tr south, and it was th tery. The spectators personally in the ma to breathe, a sound the frame of a vete era's "two" on the power them at the fin three deep around th Perry found in his ever man's eyeball th proach of a cavalry

And so enthused treated us as we dri next is going to be about after a while wish that you could

although Bobby ultimately, if incorrectly, collected the winner's cup—the first trophy he was ever to receive. At the time, she had the advantage of being twelve years old while Bobby was only six, and still they were only a stroke apart. Alexa shared Bobby's love of learning as she did his love of golf. She was a pioneer in women's golf, and later became a successful trader on Wall Street. Alexa and Bobby remained friends for the rest of their lives.

Perry and his family also played a fundamental role in Bobby's life. Bit by bit, Bobby began to add weight and muscle to his frame, and grew into a stocky youngster. The two boys played with and against each other regularly at East Lake. Bobby broke 80 for the first time the summer that he was eleven, and as the two of them honed their skills, they began entering local and regional tournaments, developing quite a reputation for themselves as the Boy Wonders. Bobby won the Atlanta Athletic Club title at age nine, and an invitational

in Birmingham, Alabama, at 13. At 14, he took the East Lake Invitational, and later that same year, Bobby and Perry were facing each other in the final round of the Georgia State Amateur, which Bobby won on the last green. At this point, George Adair, Perry's father, a great booster of local amateur golf who had done so much to support the boys' development, arranged to take Bobby with him and Perry to his first national competition, the U.S. Amateur at the Merion Cricket Club in Pennsylvania.

Merion offered Bobby his first taste of the big show. Neither the long, challenging course with its lightning-fast greens, nor the big, raucous galleries seemed to faze the boy, who made an immediate sensation. He didn't win, but he immediately caught the attention of the golf world and the press, whipping two former amateur champions before losing to the defending champ, Bob Gardner. The year was 1916, and Bobby was only fourteen, the youngest player to qualify for the tournament. Suddenly, the harsh light of public attention shone on Bobby, and with the adulation came the first hints of the discomfort and anxiety that his celebrity would cause later in life. For better or for worse, Bobby Jones was launched onto the national stage, and his career a sports icon was begun in earnest.

OPPOSITE: The Atlanta Journal *shares the community's adoration, as well as its hopes and dreams, for young Bobby.*

East Lake

The scenes of East Lake Golf Club in *Stroke of Genius* were shot at the actual club outside of Atlanta, where the clubhouse looks today much as it did when Bobby Jones played there as a boy. The club has a rich and fascinating heritage. Toward the end of the 19th century, a group of men formed the Atlanta Athletic Club in a downtown building. The club's activities, which included tennis, track, swimming and basketball, were directed by John Heisman, the Georgia Tech football coach for whom the Heisman trophy, awarded annually to college football's outstanding player, is named.

The club's membership grew quickly, and with the rising interest in golf, its leaders realized quickly that a course would be a welcome addition. The club found land in what were then the Atlanta suburbs, in East Lake, and in 1908, when Bobby Jones was just six, the course opened. The original course was only nine holes, but was later expanded to eighteen. A second course was added, and opened in 1930, the year of Bobby's Grand Slam.

Starting in the 1960s and 1970s, the neighborhood went through some transformations, as did many American urban areas at the time. The No. 2 course was sold and turned into a housing project, and East Lake went through some hard economic times. In the early 1990s, the club was purchased by a charitable foundation. A significant renewal project began, partly as a tribute to Bobby Jones and other great golfers, but also to spark a renaissance of the area.

The East Lake Club has hosted a number of major tournaments over the years, including the Ryder Cup matches of 1963, and is now home to the PGA tour's season finale championships.

INSET: A painting of the clubhouse at East Lake as it originally appeared.

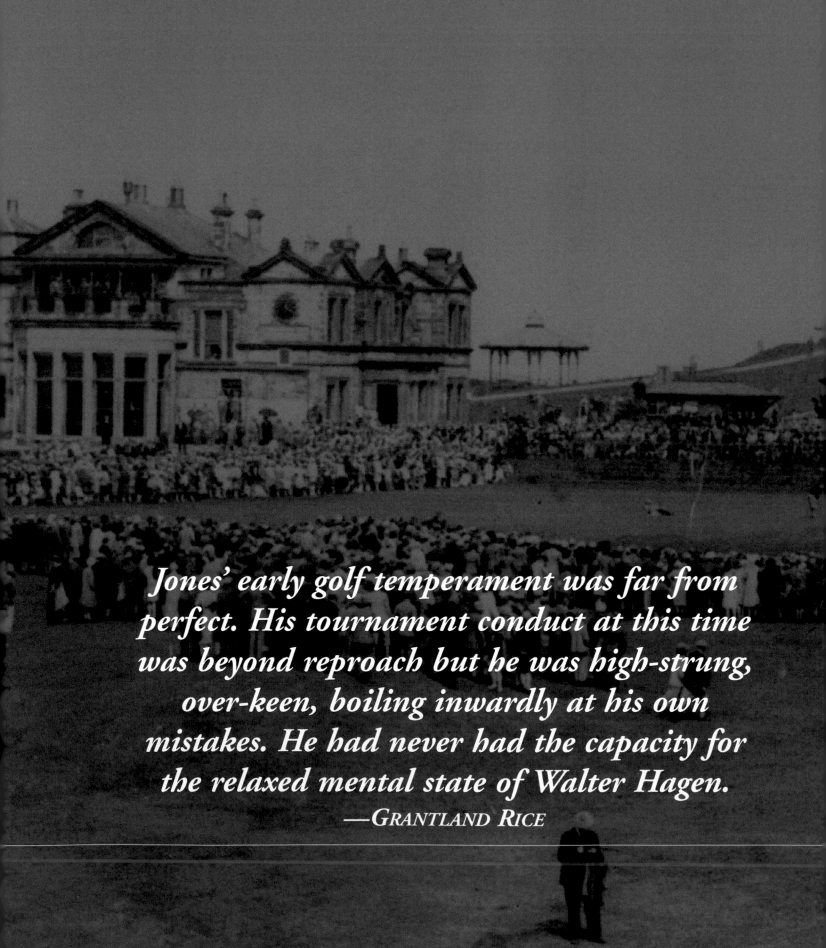

Jones' early golf temperament was far from perfect. His tournament conduct at this time was beyond reproach but he was high-strung, over-keen, boiling inwardly at his own mistakes. He had never had the capacity for the relaxed mental state of Walter Hagen.

—GRANTLAND RICE

Playing Golf

1916-1930

O.B. Keeler famously described Bobby Jones' playing career as "seven lean years and seven fat years." Starting in 1916, when Bobby competed in his first U.S. Amateur at age fourteen, he traveled across the country, playing before great crowds in major tournaments and lesser tournaments, but somehow could not find a way to win. But in 1923, when he finally broke through to take the U.S. Open at Inwood, NY, it was like opening the floodgates. From that moment until his retirement in 1930, Bobby was transformed from his era's "best player never to win a major" into the winningest golfer the world had ever known.

These years were both wonderful and treacherous for young Bobby. Here was a boy—a precocious and talented, yet thoughtful and introspective boy—growing into manhood in something of a fishbowl. To be sure, Bobby cherished his solitude and sought a sense of normalcy and routine in his life, but still he was playing golf in front of the eyes of the nation, with the hopes and dreams of his family and community resting on his shoulder. It's hard for anyone to grow up under such a spotlight, but perhaps especially hard for Bobby Jones, who aimed for perfection, and believed that it was possible to achieve, in all things, and whose courtly Southern manner and genteel articulateness masked a volcanic competitive temperament. Although he said it much later in Bobby's life than the film shows, Grantland Rice described Jones as having "the face of an angel and the temper of a timber wolf." It took Bobby the long hard years of his adolescence to quiet those demons and give himself the freedom to become a champion.

When contemplating Bobby Jones' rise to dominance on the golf course, one must never lose sight of the fact that golf was but one aspect of the young man's life during these years. Even as a boy, Bobby Jones possessed and innate sense of responsibility and seriousness of purpose. He thought about his future, and planned for it from a very early age. As much as he adored the game of golf, his worldview encompassed so much more: love and marriage,

PRECEDING SPREAD: An early round at the 1927 British Open.

family, education and professional success, and responsibility to his community. All of these facets of his character were developing at the same time, and with the same intensity, as his stature in the golfing world.

During his teens, Bobby played in a variety of tournaments, including the Southern Amateur and Western Amateur, the Canadian Open and a variety of invitational tournaments. In addition, Bobby would be invited to play exhibition matches as his notoriety and popularity increased. In 1918, when Bobby was sixteen and the nation was at war, he, Alexa Stirling, Perry Adair, and another girl named Elaine Rosenthal toured the country in a series of matches to benefit the Red Cross. He and Perry played a series of War Relief matches with two other boys that same year.

After graduating from Tech High School, at sixteen Bobby entered Georgia Tech, and began a course of study that ended in his earning a bachelor's in mechanical engineering in 1922. During these years he played for Georgia Tech's golf team, leading them to championships. While still in school, Bobby continued to play in major tournaments, including the U.S. Amateur and Open. A hint of his future back problems arose one season when he was forced to sit out with a condition doctors called "lumbago."

In 1921, Bobby made his first sojourn to the United Kingdom. Traveling overseas was a considerably greater challenge in those days than it is now. It was particularly difficult for an amateur like Jones, who was obliged to cover his trans-Atlantic crossing and other expenses out of his own resources. This first trip was packed with events, beginning with an informal match between an American team and a team of golfers from Great Britain and Ireland. This match at Hoylake, which the Americans won, was the predecessor of the Walker Cup matches, which began in earnest the following year and would become a golfing tradition. The very next day, Bobby entered his first British Amateur on the same course, and a few

(continued on page 98)

ABOVE: Bobby putts in a 1918 Red Cross match for War Relief. With him are Perry Adair, Alexa Stirling, and Elaine Rosenthal.

British Open, 1921, St. Andrews

This uncharacteristic surrender did actually take place on the Old Course at St. Andrews, during Bobby's first sojourn there, for the 1921 Open Championship. Jones' initial exposure to golf Scottish-style was like a cold slap in the face. The voracious bunkers and mysterious undulating greens were trouble some enough, but with the addition of changeable skies and diabolical gusting winds, Bobby's game simply came unglued. He took a 46 on the front nine, and after a double-bogey six on the tenth, Bobby had had enough. For the first and only time in his career, he picked up his ball, stuffed it in his pocket, and thereby withdrew from the Open. The withdrawal astonished competitors and spectators alike, but most importantly, it astonished Bobby himself. The move haunted him for years, and stood for him as a reminder always to finish whatever he had begun. He referred to the incident as his most inglorious moment, caused by his impetuous youth.

97

weeks later, stepped on to the Old Course at St. Andrews for the first time, for the 1921 British Open Championship.

This tournament, of course, is played out in great detail in *Stroke of Genius*, as it was the scene of one of the most dramatic moments in Jones' career, or as he himself put it, his "most inglorious failure." Bobby made a good enough showing over the first thirty-six holes, but on the front nine during his third round, the Old Course got the better of him, and he eventually picked up and withdrew in a pique of frustration on the eleventh hole. Almost immediately, the contemplative young man understood the mistake he had made in failing to follow through with the competition, and felt duly chastened. From that day forward, that single act stood as an object lesson not only in humility, but in the need for perseverance, a theme that run through Bobby's life.

As young men do, Bobby also pursued another dream of his heart. He had known the pretty Mary Malone for years, having been schoolmates and sporting companions with her brothers. While *Stroke of Genius* has the two meeting randomly during Bobby's college years, and falling instantly and deeply in love, in reality Mary was what O.B. Keeler called Bobby's "boyhood sweetheart." As he blossomed into adulthood, he wooed her with a singular determination, over the initial reluctance of her father to have Mary involved with a non-Catholic. The movie does indeed capture the simple truth of their relationship, which is that they were deeply and unconditionally in love, soulmates and helpmates and virtually inseparable almost from the start.

As he matured, Bobby was forced to confront and conquer his inner demons—the perfectionism that fueled his fiery temper, and the burdens of expectation and responsibility, either real or imagined, that he stoically shouldered. He never revealed the turmoil within, but Mary and O.B., the two people in the world closest to him, knew how it was eating him up. And Keeler, for one, knew how much all the angst and anxiety was getting in his way. With the help and support of such loved ones, Bobby ultimately calmed the emotional storms and prepared himself for the rendezvous with destiny that finally came in July of 1923, in the U.S. Open at Inwood Country Club, just outside of New York City on Long Island.

On the final day, Jones completed the first of two rounds played that day with a three-stroke lead, but his game began to

1923 U.S. OPEN · INWOOD C.C.

crack during the second eighteen holes. When he finished, Keeler was convinced that Jones had the tournament in hand, even though there were still contending players on the course. Jones thought otherwise, and was characteristically hard on himself, telling Keeler, "I didn't finish like a champion. I finished like a yellow dog." Jones was prescient. A young player named Bobby Cruikshank finished strong, tying Bobby and forcing an eighteen hole playoff the next day. The climactic scene of that playoff is acted out in *Stroke of Genius*. Cruikshank and Jones were even after seventeen holes, and Bobby's situation looked bleak after he hit his tee shot into the rough, a difficult lie nearly 200 yards from the green. Knowing that his opponent was also in trouble, and not being one to play things safe, Bobby took out a 2-iron and hit one of the most improbable shots of his career, a charmed and majestic approach that landed eight feet from the cup, and secured his first major-tournament victory. Finally, the terrible weight of seven years unfulfilled promise was lifted, and Bobby's life entered a new phase.

ABOVE: Jim Caviezel mulls over a scene on the 1923 U.S. Open set.
BELOW: Bobby and Mary got married on June 17, 1924.

Less than a year later, in June of 1924, Bobby and Mary were married in Atlanta. And very soon after, they began a family. In relatively short order, the couple welcomed a daughter, Clara Malone Jones; a son, Robert Tyre Jones III; and the baby girl, Mary Ellen. He earned a bachelor of arts degree in English Literature from Harvard University in 1924, and while he was ineligible to play on the golf team there because of his years at Georgia Tech, he did coach the younger players. Back home in Atlanta, he did indeed try his hand as selling real estate, working with his old chum Perry Adair. After not too long, though, he enrolled in law school at Emory. Bobby chose to take his bar exam after only one year of school and perhaps to nobody's surprise, he passed, and began what turned into a long and successful practice of law.

Amazingly, even as Bobby Jones was laying the foundation for his life as a prosperous and responsible adult, he was enjoying his greatest prolonged success on the golf course—"the fat years."

But Bobby's run didn't begin immediately. He lost a playoff match in the 1925 U.S. Open when he declared a one-stroke penalty on himself after seeing his ball move slightly as he addressed it. The film is true to the actual event, in that neither his competitors nor the tournament officials saw the ball move, nor were they insisting on the penalty. It was Bobby who refused to let the inadvertent infraction pass, and sure enough, when he was praised—unjustly, he

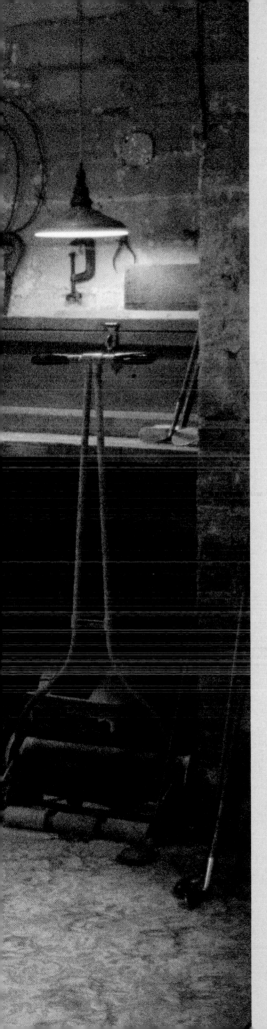

The Swing

The fabled swing of Bobby Jones looked graceful and effortless, but was extraordinarily powerful. Jones was among the longest hitters of his day, using roughly made clubs with hickory shafts, half a century before the advent of graphite and titanium. Jones was neither tall nor lean, but hitched his left knee in on his backswing as many golfers did at the time, which helped him achieve a full turn of his hips and shoulders, often bringing his club back past parallel. Once at the top, he'd plant his left heel and begin his strong, fluid downswing, ending with a classic high finish.

All three actors who played Jones studied films, and worked with a series of professional golf instructors so they could each master the swing of Bobby Jones, which is instantly recognizable to golf aficionados. It came most easily to Thomas Lewis, who was already a seasoned golfer. Devon Gearhart also managed a creditable imitation. Like Jones himself when he was child, Devon is a natural mimic who enjoyed learning to replicate Jones' motion. Jim Caviezel worked the hardest, and came the farthest, having played almost no golf before signing on to *Stroke of Genius*. But arguably, there was more riding on his performance. The character's adult swing was sure to be scrutinized for authenticity, and Caviezel's success is as impressive an athletic achievement as it is a dramatic one.

believed—for his integrity, he replied, "You might as well praise a man for not robbing a bank." Moments like this have passed into lore, and are part of the enduring Jones legend. Bobby did win the U.S. Amateur in both 1924 and 1925.

In 1926, Jones won the British Open at Muirfield, which included a stunning, near-perfect round of 66 on an extremely challenging course, a round which he himself called, "the best round I ever played in competition." Upon his return to New York, Jones was honored with a Broadway ticker-tape parade. Shortly after, Bobby went to Columbus, Ohio for the U.S. Open, which he also won, making him the first golfer ever to win both Open championships in the same year—the "double" that would foreshadow his Grand Slam a few years later.

And then in 1927, Bob returned to St. Andrews, the scene of his ignoble withdrawal years before. This time, he claimed the Claret Jug, winning the Open Championship for the second year in a row, and permanently securing the affection of golf fans there by publicly declaring that the Cup itself would remain in St. Andrews during his reign as champion. Over the next two years, Bobby won a U.S. Open and took second in another, took one more U.S. Amateur, and played for a victorious Walker Cub team as he honed his skills in preparation for the great climax of his career.

BELOW: Jones on the first tee on the Old Course at St. Andrews.

Over the winter of 1930, Bob Jones very quietly and privately turned his attention on the possibility of doing something that no other golfer had ever done—winning all four major championships in the same year. In his day, that meant the Amateur and Open championships of both the United States and Great Britain. (Today, a grand slam refers to the U.S. Open, the British Open, the PGA Championship, and Jones' own tournament, the Masters.) For the first time in his playing career, Bob worked out in the cold months, keeping himself fit and focused. He played in a pair or warm-up tournaments in the South in the early spring, one of which, the Southern Open, he won handily, before heading across the Atlantic.

It is often forgotten that in early May of 1930, Bob played on America's winning team in the Walker Cup

matches at Royal St. George's. Ironically, he may never have even made it to England that historic year. After the Walker Cup, Jones claimed the British Amateur at his beloved St. Andrews, besting Roger Wethered in the final round. Less than a month later he won his third British Open at Hoylake. In June, he triumphed at Interlachen in Minnesota for his fourth U.S. Open title, and finally, in September, Bobby returned to Merion Cricket Club in Pennsylvania, the site of his first appearance in a U.S. Amateur, his first national tournament, not quite fifteen years before. Bobby trounced his opponent, Eugene Homans, in the final round, claiming his fifth national amateur crown.

For months, this shy, quiet and bookish young man from Atlanta basked in—he might have said "suffered through"—the world's adulation. He was feted both at home and abroad, and hailed in New York City with his second ticker-tape parade. Exhausted yet satisfied—content, even—Robert Tyre Jones, Jr. made an announcement that stunned the world. Having privately come to the realization that there were no worlds left for him to conquer in golf, he retired from competition. Bobby returned to his Atlanta home, and though he remained a fixture in the golfing community for the rest of his life, he now assumed the mantle of full-time husband, father, and working man. Perhaps Bobby's competitors breathed a collective sigh of relief, but to be sure, a remarkable era in sports had ended.

PRECEDING SPREAD: The scene at St. Andrews after Bobby's second British Open victory. BELOW: Jones is the only person to be celebrated twice with ticker-tape parades in lower Manhattan.

Mashies and Niblicks

One of the more charming elements of this bygone era in golf is the archaic golf club nomenclature. Throughout the film, players can be heard talking about such oddities as mashies and brassies and niblicks, since this was before the introduction of mass-produced numbered clubs with steel shafts. A quick guide to some of the lingo and the modern equivalents:

Brassie: 2-wood
Spoon: 3-wood
Cleek: 1-iron
Mid-mashie: 3-iron
Mashie: 5-iron
Mashie-Niblick: 7-iron
Niblick: 9-iron (also sometimes called a Baffing-Spoon)

Bobby Jones carried a few dearly beloved clubs, which have become legendary among aficionados. True to his literary nature, he nicknamed his driver "Jeannie Deans" after a Walter Scott heroine, and used it to win many championships. And his famous putter, first given to him by Stewart Maiden's brother Jim, was called "Calamity Jane." Later, when Bobby worried that the old putter's scarred and pitted face might cause him some problems, he had it copied, and called his new one "Calamity Jane II."

Also, just as baseball had its "dead-ball era" before the introduction of the current lively ball, golf at the beginning of the century used what was known as the "gutta-percha" ball, made of a natural latex from exotic Asian trees. They were easy to control, but did not last very long. Bobby Jones began playing at roughly the same time that the world of golf was converting to a new kind of ball, with a tightly wound rubber-banded interior. This was, of course, a happy coincidence for Bobby, who was known as one of the longer hitters of his day.

OPPOSITE: Bobby Jones at nineteen. ABOVE: Jones' actual clubs from 1928. BELOW: Prop clubs used during filming. Photo courtesy of Linda Priddy.

With all the physical qualifications, Jones had an unusually fine brain and unusual determination and courage. But he had always had the high-strung temperament that goes better in football and tennis than it goes in golf—the yearning for action rather than the feeling of restraint and never control.

—GRANTLAND RICE

Grantland Rice

The Best at *His* Game

Grantland Rice has been called the best-loved American sports writer of all time, and is the standard against which all others are compared. Early in his career he worked in the South, including, coincidentally, Atlanta, but really made his mark when he came to New York. He had a way with a turn of phrase, and could create drama out of the most ordinary athletic match-ups. Just as his dubbing of Notre Dame's starting backfield as "The Four Horsemen" passed into football legend, much of the versifying with which he peppered his columns has become all but immortal. The most memorable, of course, is a couplet from his poem, "Alumnus Football":

For when the one great Scorer comes to write against your name,
He marks—not that you won or lost—but how you played the game.

Rice did not pen those lines about Bobby Jones, nor even about golf, but the words unquestionably make us think of Bobby's unique mixture of competitive fire, humility, and pure enjoyment of the game.

Rice is associated with a period that has been referred to as a golden age in American sports. In the years between the two World Wars, college athletics, where scholar-athletes were still the ideal, captivated the public's attention; and professional sports (dominated at the time by baseball) had not yet become the overblown spectacles of today. Before television took over, the American public depended on newspaper scribes like Rice to set the exciting sports stories of the day into words. Rice and his colleagues—who included the likes of Ring Lardner and Damon Runyon—turned athletes into mythic heroes, and transformed their exploits into folklore. They were indispensable to the popularity of sports, and became important national celebrities in their own right. Rice not only wrote about Bobby Jones, but helped educate Americans about all the sports legends of the era, from Babe Ruth to Babe Didrikson.

ABOVE: Bob is congratulated by Grantland Rice, right, after winning the U.S. Open in 1923. LEFT: Allen O'Reilly as Rice.

No. 9X

Price 35 Cents

SPALDING'S
ATHLETIC LIBRARY

GOLF Guide 1931

Robert Tyre Jones Jr.

Edited by
GRANTLAND RICE

American Sports Publishing Company 45 Rose St. New York

UNITED STATES AMATEUR CHAMPION
1924 1925 1927 1928 1930

UNITED STATES OPEN CHAMPION
1923 1926 1929 1930

BRITISH AMATEUR CHAMPION
1930

BRITISH OPEN CHAMPION
1926 1927 1930

Harry Vardon
The Old Master

Harry Vardon was the first great name in modern golf. Born on the British isle of Jersey in 1870, Vardon grew up playing a modified version of the game with homemade clubs on a miniature course. His introduction to serious golf came as it did to so many others, as a caddy for for a local gentleman. Slowly, Vardon began entering—and eventually winning—a variety of golf tournaments. Over the course of his career, he won dozens and dozens of tournaments, but his most astonishing accomplishment was his six British Open victories, a record that has yet to be matched. It is not known for certain whether or not Vardon actually invented the overlapping grip that now bears his name, but without doubt he made it popular. The Vardon grip is still used today. In that time, pros knew they were likely to earn more money barnstorming in the U.S., and Vardon came here often, playing exhibition matches and major tournaments. It was at one of these exhibitions, at East Lake Country Club, where a young Bobby Jones first saw Vardon play, as the film depicts. Over twenty years, Vardon added a couple of U.S. Open victories to his memorable record.

For Americans, Vardon is probably best remembered not for his many victories, but for one resounding defeat. At the 1913 US Open, played in Brookline, Massachusetts, Vardon, recognized internationally as the greatest golfer of the day, was unquestionably the man to beat. And that's exactly what an unknown named Francis Ouimet did. Ouimet was a 20-year-old working-class kid who also picked up the game while caddying, in his case at the Brookline Country Club where the Open was held. It is said that Ouimet's victory over Vardon and Ted Ray, the other great professional of the day, jump-started golf's popularity in America. Ouimet's impact was much like Greg LeMond's and Lance Armstrong's in cycling, or the international success of the U.S. Women's Soccer Team.

Bobby's official introduction to Harry Vardon came at Jones' first British Open, played in 1921 on the hallowed ground of St. Andrews in Scotland. The scene in the movie in which Bobby asks Vardon, "Have you ever seen a worse shot than that?" and receives a curt "No" in response is based on fact. The story has been handed down for generations as a key moment in golf lore.

ABOVE: Bobby with the great Harry Vardon, at Jones' first U.S. Open in 1920, at Toledo, Ohio. OPPOSITE: Aidan Quinn as Harry Vardon putts on the 18th-hole green of the Old Course at St. Andrews.

The Golden Age of Sport

In the prime of his competitive career, Bobby Jones was arguably the most revered and celebrated athlete in the country. His Grand Slam earned him a prodigious ticker-tape parade through the canyons of lower Manhattan, a reception reserved for only the most beloved national heroes. Bobby's fame and lofty status is especially impressive when one considers the other legendary athletes who were competing for the public's attention in those years, which have been called by some a "golden age" in American sports.

At Yankee Stadium in New York, Babe Ruth was patrolling right field and anchoring "Murderer's Row," a lineup that included Lou Gehrig, Tony Lazzeri, Earle Combs and Bob Meusel. The Yankees of 1927, one of the greatest teams in the history of the game, had a winning percentage that was well over .700, and took the American League by a staggering margin of 19 games. Elsewhere in baseball, Cleveland had the great Tris Speaker, and Ty Cobb was tearing things up in Detroit.

In those days, college football was king. It was the era of Knute Rockne's championship teams at Notre Dame, featuring a fabled backfield dubbed by Grantland Rice the "Four Horseman." And fewer football stars were better known than the Galloping Ghost, Red Grange of Illinois. A perennial All-American, Grange secured his place in history by powering his team over Michigan—their first defeat in three years. When Grange went on to play for the Chicago Bears in the fledgling NFL, his fame helped put pro football on the map.

Boxing legends Jack Dempsey and Gene Tunney slugged it out in an epic bout before 150,000 fans in Chicago's Soldier Field, and the flamboyant Bill Tilden dominated the world of tennis, winning every major title he sought and representing the U.S. on every Davis Cup team between 1920 and 1930.

But American's weren't only watching the men. This was the time of the indomitable Mildred "Babe" Didrikson, perhaps the greatest female athlete in American history.

Babe won gold and silver medals in track and field at the 1932 Olympics. She was an All-American basketball player. In truth, she became expert at just about every sport she tried, including baseball, tennis, diving and bowling. But it was not until she took up golf that her legend was secured. She was the first woman to win both the US and British Amateur titles and won every professional title available to women. Bobby Jones called her one of the ten best golfers of all time, male or female.

The list goes on and on, of course, but in this pantheon of sporting heroes, none ranked above Bobby Jones, whose skill claimed the respect and admiration of millions, and whose integrity and good grace won their hearts.

ABOVE: Lou Gehrig and Babe Ruth of the 1927 New York Yankees. OPPOSITE: Babe Didrikson.

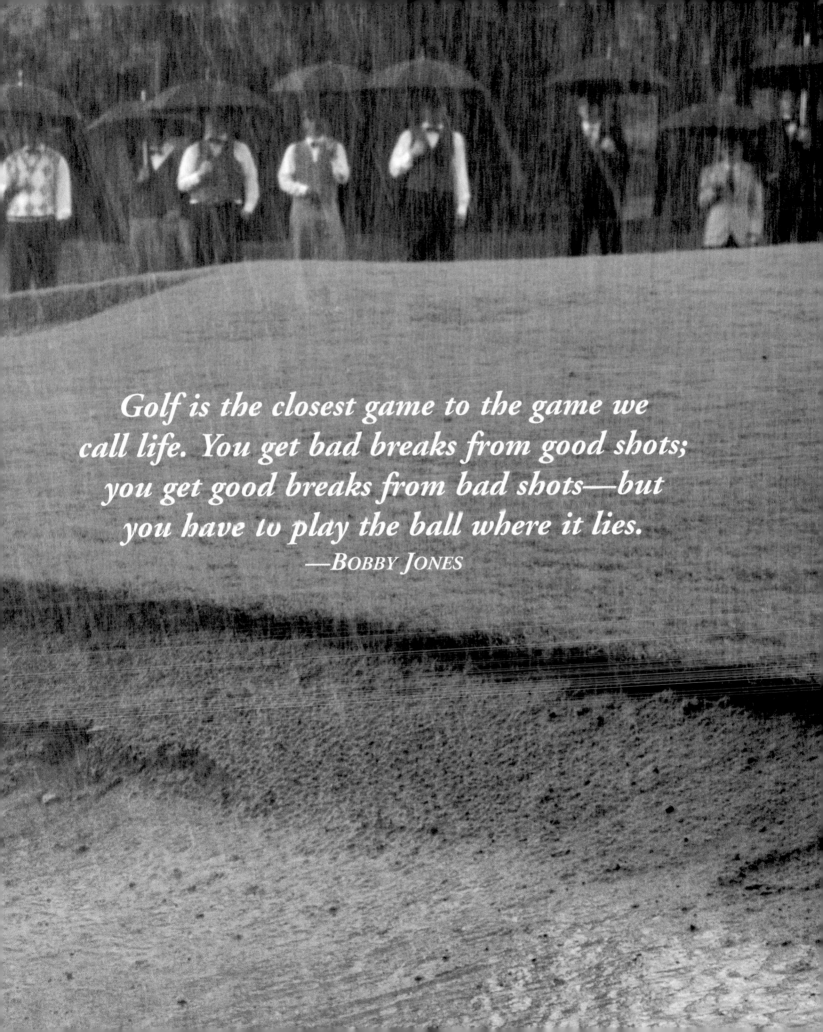

Golf is the closest game to the game we call life. You get bad breaks from good shots; you get good breaks from bad shots—but you have to play the ball where it lies.
—BOBBY JONES

Walter Hagen
"Sir Walter," The Dapper Pro

Walter Hagen was not only the most flamboyant character in American golf, but one of the most colorful characters in the world of sports. His great record in golf was always overshadowed by his outsized personality and his outrageous antics. That's saying quite a lot, considering that Hagen's numerous successes encompassed two U.S Opens, four British Opens, five PGA Championships (four of which were won in consecutive years, a feat unmatched since), and forty PGA Tour victories.

Hagen came from modest means, a blacksmith's son from Rochester, New York, who first came to golf through the caddie's entrance. By age thirteen, Hagen had left school, and by nineteen was the head pro at The Country Club of Rochester. He began testing the waters of tournament play, and quickly built a record of success. Hagen's scrappy play reflects his upbringing. Throughout his playing career, his success depended on his uncanny ability to get out of trouble with brilliant recovery shots, what golfers today call "scrambling." But wherever he went, win or lose, "The Haig" left his indelible mark. As a young man, he would inspire giggles among his competitors by showing up in garish outfits, but would soon quiet their laughter with his skillful play and competitive fire. As Hagen matured, his public persona took on a new quality, evolving from the cocky hick to outgoing, confident showman. Hagen's antics might have earned lesser men a reputation for obnoxiousness or even a few black eyes, but fans and competitors alike delighted in Hagen's way with a crowd, and his unwavering sense that some things shouldn't be taken too seriously.

Once, in a tournament playoff, Hagen escaped defeat in classic fashion. On the next-to-last hole, his errant drive ended up buried in soft dirt. There was no easy way to recover from such a terrible lie, and the extra stroke or two would likely cost Hagen the tournament. Even though the playoff was a match-play

ABOVE: Bobby Jones, left, and Walter Hagen, 1926.

format, meaning that there was only one other player on the course at the time, Hagen invoked a rule that allowed him to inspect the ball to insure it was his. He calmly picked it up out of the dirt and made quite a long show of carefully inspecting the ball, taking enough time for the hole to fill back up, giving Hagen the lie he needed to make a great recovery shot and get back in the game.

Those in the know credit Hagen with another fundamental transformation in the game of golf. When he broke into the game, it was still primarily a game for society's elite. Professional golfers were held in low esteem, ranked somewhere near riverboat gamblers in social status. Most of the finer golf clubs wouldn't even allow pros to use the members' entrances or facilities. Hagen, who had become wealthy playing the game, would have none of it. One of the most oft-told stories about Walter Hagen tells of his camping out in a chauffeur-driven Rolls-Royce during the 1930 British Open, on account of his being denied entrance to the front door of the club. He had sumptuous meals served to him in the back seat of the Rolls, all the while remaining parked in front of the clubhouse. The British press took the "boorish" American to task, but he soon won them over with his charm and his solid play. On another occasion, he refused to enter a clubhouse to receive his trophy because he had not been allowed admittance earlier. Years later, Arnold Palmer, whose impact on the game was considerable, paid tribute to Hagen at a dinner in his honor: "If not for you, Walter, this dinner would be downstairs in the pro shop, not in the ballroom."

Hagen, along with Babe Ruth, ushered in the age of the sports celebrity, making a fortune from product endorsements and appearance fees, and generally living large, all of which earned him the nickname "Sir Walter." Always eager for the attention and affection of the public, Hagen memorably said, "I never wanted to be a millionaire. I just wanted to live like one."

Hagen makes more bad shots in a single season than Harry Vardon did from 1890 to 1914, but he beats more immaculate golfers because, "three of those and one of them counts four," and he knows it.
—A. C. CROOME

What we are left with in the end is a forever young, good-looking Southerner, an impeccably courteous and decent man with a private ironical view of life who, to the great good fortune of people who saw him, happened to play the great game with more magic and more grace than anyone before or since.
—ALISTAIR COOKE

Life After Golf

In the years immediately following his Grand Slam victory, Bobby retired into the workaday life of a happy family man. It took some time for the public's fascination with him to cool, but Bobby, innately a private man to begin with, kept his gaze fixed firmly on his family and his business. The one significant exception, of course, was his involvement with Clifford Roberts and their quest to build a championship-caliber golf club in the South, and to attract a major tournament there. The story is well known by now: The club they envisioned became Augusta National, and their tournament, The Masters.

Bob threw himself into the practice of law just as he had thrown himself into every facet of his life previously—golf, education, marriage, fatherhood. His practice flourished, and his firm, although it no longer bears his name, is still active in Atlanta today. In addition to his involvement with Augusta, Jones kept his hand in the golf world in a number of ways. He wrote several books on golf, mostly instructionals, in collaboration with his old friend and confidante, O.B. Keeler. He signed on with Warner Brothers, for a tidy six-figure sum that he donated to charity, for a series of short instructional films, some of which featured Hollywood stars of that era, including W.C. Fields, Loretta Young and Harold Lloyd, with all of whom Bobby could hold his own. Viewing these films, one experiences the gracious manner and quiet confidence that so many have described. They are available as videos, and DVDs now, and are even shown occasionally on cable television.

Bobby oversaw the opening of the Augusta National Golf Club in 1933, and the next year he played, somewhat reluctantly, in the inaugural Masters tournament, called at that time The Augusta National Invitation Tournament. Not having played competitively in four years, Bobby put up a respectable 294 and tied for 13th place. He would play in ten more Masters tournaments, perhaps more out of his ties to the club and the golfing community than out of any still-smoldering competitiveness. He was never really in serious contention.

The calmness of Bobby's new life wasn't seriously disrupted until the Second

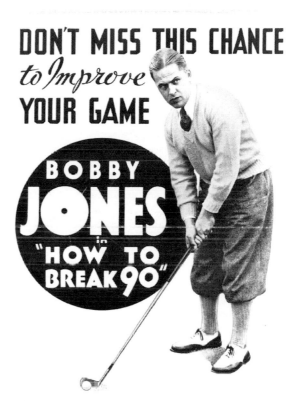

OPPOSITE: Bobby making one of his Warner Brothers films. ABOVE: An advertising poster for his short films. PRECEDING SPREAD (from left to right): Ben Lyon, director George E. Marshall, Bobby Jones, and Bebe Daniels on the set of one of Bobby Jones Warner Brothers films.

World War broke out. Like many other great athletes of his day—Ted Williams, Joe DiMaggio, Gene Tunney, and Jesse Owens, to name a few—Jones gave himself over to the greater good and joined the Armed Forces. Some were obliged to serve during their prime playing years, but not Bobby. His age and medical condition would have exempted him, but he signed up anyway, sensing yet another opportunity to contribute, to do the right thing. Bobby was commissioned a captain in 1942 and at first assigned to help oversee the observation posts along the Atlantic seaboard. Later, he was promoted to major and posted to London as an intelligence officer. When his group was converted to infantry, he landed with them at Normandy on D-Day-plus-one, spending time in the line of fire. Jones returned from Europe and the service of General Eisenhower some months later, having attained the rank of lieutenant colonel.

Later, Dwight D. Eisenhower became a fixture at Augusta National and good friend to both Jones and Clifford Roberts. There is still today a cottage on the club grounds, called the Eisenhower Cottage, that was built to accommodate the then President and his entourage, and which now serves as a broadcast facility during the Masters. Jones and Roberts both served Eisenhower as advisers during later political campaigns.

In the late forties, the periodic health problems—the aches and pains, the varicose veins, the troubles with his extremities—that had plagued Bobby in his younger days began to get more chronic and severe. A good friend, Tommy Barnes, reported playing a round with him at East Lake, and watching Bob hit the only bad drive this friend had ever seen. Jones finished the round at even par, but never played another complete round again. Abnormalities in his spine were detected, and over the next several years, the pain spread and intensified throughout his body. None of the treatments and surgeries that doctors tried seemed to help, and by the mid-1950s it was determined that Bobby was suffering from a rare degenerative neurological disorder called syringomyelia. (*See page 148.*) Although treatment of the disease has come a long way since Bob Jones' day, his was so far advanced by the time that the diagnosis was confirmed that there was little that could be done for him.

Bobby stayed as active and involved as his condition would allow over the next decade and a half, but he was confined by braces and crutches and eventually a wheelchair. Pain was his constant companion, but it was neither a subject

ABOVE: Bobby arrives at St. Andrews to be honored with the Freedom of the City in 1958. OPPOSITE: Captain Jones during the Second World War.

130

for conversation nor an excuse for self-pity. Just as Bob had never ballyhooed his own achievements in golf or in business, and had never spent much time telling war stories, he never called attention to his condition, or made apologies for it.

Near the end of his life, Robert Tyre Jones, Jr. returned to Scotland, to St. Andrews. The trip was a profound emotional moment, both for Bobby and his hosts, and a fitting bookend for a man whose character was in part forged on the Old Course fifty years before. The town had invited Bob back to honor him. In a memorable ceremony, during which he was first honored and then humbly returned both the praise and true affection in his own address, Bobby was given "The Freedom of the Royal Burgh of St. Andrews," an honor bestowed previously on only one other American: Benjamin Franklin.

As Claire Forlani points out, Bobby converted to Catholicism in his last days, a final testament to his love for Mary. A week after, on December 18, 1971, his life slipped away quietly while he slept. Play stopped on the Old Course when news of Bobby's passing reached St. Andrews, and the clubhouse flag was lowered to half-mast. One year later, a ceremonial silver golf club was paraded through the "Old Toon," signaling a memorial church service. Later that day, a plaque was unveiled on the tenth hole, officially naming it "The Bobby Jones Hole."

Bob's contribution to our great game is reflected by its deserved prominence in the field of sports, but his gift to his friends is the warmth that comes from unselfishness, superb judgment, nobility of character and unwavering loyalty of principle.
—PRESIDENT DWIGHT D. EISENHOWER

OPPOSITE: Jones in later life.

St. Andrews
The Home of Golf

Golfers speak its name in hushed, reverential tones. Tennis has Wimbledon, baseball has the House that Ruth Built, cycling has Alpe d'Huez —the ultimate test, the pinnacle of achievement, the crucible in which legends are forged. None are older, or more hallowed, than the Old Course at St. Andrews, an ancient town on Scotland's eastern coast.

Golf has been played over this rolling, windswept landscape for six hundred years, interrupted periodically by such episodes as the sport being banned by King James II of Scotland. By the 19th century, golf had become integral to the local culture, and an anchor of the local economy. Although St. Andrews now boasts six full golf courses, it is the fabled Old Course that golfers revere. Its small but deep and voracious pot bunkers, treacherous undulating greens, and rugged ungroomed rough have been the very definition of "links-style" golf for generations. But it is the brisk and blustery climate that makes St. Andrews, like most Scottish links, so diabolically challenging. The random gusts of wind and the seemingly ever-present mist and dampness chill golfers to the bone and make every round an unpredictable adventure.

According to golfing lore, the conventional eighteen-hole golf course has its origin at St. Andrews. Originally, St. Andrews had but eleven holes, and players played them twice in order to make up a full round of twenty-two holes. At one point, the local golfers determined to lengthen the first four holes into two holes, thus reducing the number to nine, which they continued to play both out and in. Later, an additional nine holes were added. Eighteen holes is now the international standard.

St. Andrews is not only the historical home of golf, but also the literal home. The Royal and Ancient Golf Club, built here in 1754 and originally called the Society of St. Andrews Golfers, is now the governing body for competitive golf around the world. (In the United States only, the United States Golf Association, or USGA, serves that function.) The R&A, as it is called, administers the rules,

ABOVE: Bobby Jones at the British Open 1927.

dictates what changes or technological advancements will be incorporated into the game, and oversees national and international tournaments. The Open Championship—what Americans call the British Open—was established by the R&A in 1860 and first played on the Old Course in 1873.

St. Andrews figures prominently in the Bobby Jones' story, of course. He first traveled to the UK in 1921, at the age of nineteen. After playing in the British Amateur, he went on to try his first British Open, played that year on the Old Course. This tournament proved to be a critical turning point in Bobby's golfing career. The course and the conditions combined to demoralize him. After a miserable front nine and a double-bogey on the tenth, he hit into a bunker on the eleventh, and decided right then and there he had enough, picked up his ball and withdrew from the competition. Later he called it his "most inglorious failure" in golf, but the brush with adversity strengthened him. He came back to England and won the Open Championship in 1926, and returned to defend the title at St. Andrews in 1927, and in the process, clear his memory of the painful disappointment there six years earlier. At the time, tradition had it that the defending champion would bring the Open trophy—the "Claret Jug"—back to St. Andrews to pass it along to the new champion, Jones captured the hearts of the citizenry by declaring that he'd insist the trophy remain in St. Andrews should he win the tournament. The film captures the magical moment many years later when Bobby returned to St. Andrews to become only the second American (the first being Ben Franklin) to be granted the "Freedom of the City," essentially becoming an honorary citizen of the town. On the day of Bobby's passing, play was stopped on the Old Course as the clubhouse flag was lowered to half-mast.

The cast and crew—and ultimately the viewers—of *Stroke of Genius* were blessed with great good fortune when they received permission to film on the course at St. Andrews. Some even went so far as to say that their decision to participate in the film was helped by this once-in-a-lifetime opportunity. Malcolm McDowell comments:

> You know, they promised me golf and, my God, they delivered on that. I played the Old Course in St. Andrews, which is one of the most delightful things I think you could ever do. It was such a great

afternoon. We went out late, 3:30 in the afternoon, and I'd just stepped off a plane from L.A. so I was jet-lagged beyond belief. And we played the Old Course. We had a wonderful Scottish caddy who was saying, "Now, you see that bush? You hit it over there, laddie." And I'm like, "What bush?" It's like there's thousands of bushes. It was so exciting. We came to the 17th, which is the Road Hole, one of the most famous holes in golf. It's where it all started. It's hallowed ground.

Time has not changed St. Andrews very much. Producer Kim Dawson marveled at how much it looks as it must have to Bobby Jones:

It's exactly as it was. The city of St. Andrews and all the buildings around it. We had to add the cars and costumes, but the setting itself is exactly as it was. The R&A hasn't changed noticeably. Maybe the golf course is somewhat different—they have irrigation now but I think you're not going to have to go too far to believe that this is period.

Walter Hagen would bark at his fellow pros, "We've got to stop this kid." Tommy Armour, the 1927 U.S. Open champion, lost several friendly matches with Jones before accepting 1 up a side in their bets. Asked years later how he could do that with an amateur, Armour growled, "Because that's how goddam good he was."
—DAVE ANDERSON

Augusta National
Jones' Legacy to American Golf

Bobby Jones' travels in the world of golf had taken him to the golfing shrine of St. Andrews, and the storied courses of the northeast, like Baltusrol, Merion and Brookline. In the end, however, Jones always came home, to Georgia, to the South. His journeys kindled inside him a simple idea: Why couldn't the South be home to a great championship golf course? To build such a course became Jones' dream, but it wasn't until after he retired from tournament golf that the dream had any hope of becoming reality.

As dynamic an individual as Bobby Jones was, the club was too big a dream for him to realize on his own. He soon became partners with Clifford Roberts, a financial operator with social ambitions. Roberts was a self-made man from a hardscrabble Midwestern upbringing. In contrast to Jones who held graduate degrees in literature and the law, Roberts had little formal education, but was a quick study with an incisive and focused intellect. Despite, or perhaps owing to, the differences in their backgrounds, the two men complemented each other perfectly. Jones, whose international celebrity was balanced by his courtly manner and educated gentility, could charm crowds and serve as the magnet for capital and recognition, while Roberts' scrappy and single-minded devotion to the project not only got it off the ground, but kept it going against difficult odds, even saving the club from the brink of dissolution on more than one occasion in the early days. The two men shared one characteristic, though, and that was an unwavering commitment to quality. Their shared perfectionism and eye for the minutest detail is what made Augusta National unique among such establishments, and in turn made the annual Masters Tournament an instant classic—one of the premier events in all of sports.

Jones and Roberts most likely got to know each other in the 1920s, when Jones was in the middle of his illustrious playing career, and Roberts was working the connections that golf was likely to offer. They brainstormed a number of possible locations for the club before finally settling on a large tract of land in

ABOVE: Bobby Jones circa 1932, during the construction of Augusta. OPPOSITE: Bobby Jones' last round at Augusta, 1948.

ABOVE: Thirteenth green at Augusta National Golf Club. OPPOSITE: Aerial view of Augusta National Golf Club.

Augusta, Georgia, about 150 miles east of Atlanta. The land had once been a family-owned plantation that had fallen on hard times and eventually was taken over by a nursery company called Fruitland. There was a small but impressive manor house on the property that eventually served as the clubhouse.

The initial plan was to use the proceeds from initial membership sales to finance the construction of the course and club. Roberts and Jones felt confident that memberships would sell quickly; the fees were inexpensive, and who would pass up the opportunity to rub shoulders with the great Bobby Jones? But this was 1931, the nadir of the Great Depression, and the first membership drive proved disastrous, despite Herculean efforts from Roberts and Jones, and even with help from the likes of Grantland Rice, himself a major national celebrity. Although the club's treasury was shored up in the early days by a handful of the more wealthy members, the initial plans, which included the construction of a new clubhouse, had to be drastically scaled back. It wasn't until after 1950, when the club was on more solid financial footing, that significant renovations to the clubhouse were undertaken.

Jones knew from the very start of the project that he wanted the course to be designed by Alister MacKenzie. MacKenzie was an Englishman of Scottish ancestry who had demonstrated a flair for golf-course design. Jones had become familiar with MacKenzie's work while playing some of his courses in California, most notably the well-known Cypress Point course. Once the club felt confident enough in its finances to commit to course construction, the actual work was completed with amazing swiftness, and Jones was able to play his first informal round within several months in 1932. Even still, times were so hard at first that MacKenzie ultimately received only a tiny fraction of his promised fee.

Interestingly, the original plans for Augusta National included the development of several building lots on the site, but as late as the 1940s and early 1950s, Roberts was unable to find any takers for these parcels of land. It's impossible for contemporary golf fans to understand, but even real-estate speculators failed to consider it an attractive proposition at the time. Years later, Clifford Roberts—

and probably the entire golfing world—came to view this lack of interest as a stroke of great fortune. It's hard to imagine this graceful and fabled course ringed with private homes or condominiums.

The club officially opened in January of 1933, an event which was marked with a special, train-board party for new members from New York to Augusta that culminated in a weekend of golf with Jones himself and his special guest, Francis Ouimet. The club endured money problems for a long time, even though the tradition of the Masters had begun immediately. During the Second World War, Jones and Roberts suspended their annual tournament and used the course to graze a herd of cattle and to raise turkeys, both to support the war effort and to bolster their precarious finances. In the relative calm of the post-war boom, the club, and its identifying tournament, both took hold in the popular imagination.

One factor that contributed to this improvement was the association with the club of Dwight D. Eisenhower. Ike first visited the club in 1948, long before he was even a candidate for the presidency, but while his war record was still fresh in the minds of Americans, who loved him as a bona fide hero. He was immediately taken with the club, and the new friends he was able to make there. Just as importantly, Augusta provided for Ike the same kind of haven that Bobby Jones had discovered there—a place for golf and friendship in a quiet and beautiful setting, far from the spotlight and hurly-burly of their national celebrity. Clifford Roberts and Augusta National played important parts in Ike's life. Its members were supporters and sometimes significant contributors to his political campaigns, and Roberts became not only the Eisenhower family's financial advisor, but also a trusted friend and confidante who was with Ike at the moment of his election to the presidency. One of the cottages on the grounds of Augusta was built with Ike's entourage in mind, and still bears the Eisenhower name. It's at the top of the list of relationships that have gone down in the lore of the club.

Jones is intertwined with the clay soil of Augusta as the giant roots of the great oak trees. His spirit lives in the towering pines, and there is a palpable sense of him in every corner of the place, each spring when his dream comes back to life during Masters week.
—LARRY DORMAN

The Masters

A Championship for the South

ABOVE: Bobby Jones portrait, wearing his Masters jacket. OPPOSITE: Panoramic view of sixteenth green action.

At the time that Augusta National opened its doors, no major national golf tournament had been played farther south than Illinois. This was, in fact one of the circumstances that drove Bobby Jones' ambition to build a championship-caliber course in Georgia. Bobby wanted to attract the serious golfers of America to his part of the country. The story of the birth of this most prestigious golfing event is a curious one.

In 1933, Clifford Roberts began talking with key national golf officials about bringing an upcoming U.S. Open to Augusta National. A major tournament was exactly what the young club needed to attract the attention and respect of the golfing world, and the nation at large. But it quickly became clear that hosting the Open posed a number of challenges. Optimal weather around Augusta was in the early spring, but the system of qualifying tournaments (which were all played in the northern states) for the Open was scheduled to accommodate a summer championship. The other reason that an Open at Augusta would have been problematic was Bobby Jones himself. Bobby had retired from tournament golf. While he still cherished the principle of amateurism, his income from golf (books and instructional films, as well as from the equipment manufacturer Spalding) had become substantial since his retirement, and to compete, he would have almost certainly had to declare himself a professional in order to play in the tournament. And everyone agreed that Jones' presence in the field would be necessary to legitimize holding the tournament in Augusta.

The point became moot when the USGA decided against having an Open at Augusta, but that turned out to be a good thing for all concerned. Clifford Roberts quickly began to think about having a private tournament at the club. Such a tournament could still include Bobby, without threatening his amateur status, and thus attracting the best golfers in the world to Augusta. Jones, of course, was somewhat reluctant to play, having been out of competitive golf for several years, but he did not feel he could invite golf's elite to play at his club if he did not intend to play himself. The golfing establishment (the USGA and the PGA), which had suffered during the depression along with the rest of the country, would benefit indirectly but immeasurably by the hoopla created by the game's biggest star returning to competitive play.

Invitations went out to the top pros, most of whom accepted, but many of whom begged off. A week's worth of activities and events were planned, and media began pumping up the tournament as a major sporting and cultural event—the Second Coming of Bobby Jones. O.B. Keeler and Grantland Rice, who was named the honorary chairman of the first tournament, both used their national platforms to draw attention to the festivities.

Naturally, all this hoopla made the modest Bobby Jones uncomfortable. His single biggest objection was with Roberts' suggested name for the tournament:

The Masters. Bobby considered this the epitome of hubris, given that he himself was the host of the tournament. The name ultimately presented to the public was "The Augusta National Invitation Tournament," although almost immediately, the press and public alike latched onto the Masters name. In 1939, the tournament was officially renamed The Masters.

Jones was never really in contention in that first tournament, but found that his fans were happy simply to see him out on the course, and the warmth of the reception he received brought him back for many years to come. The inaugural tournament was won by Horton Smith, but it was not until the following year, that an extraordinary event truly put the tournament on the map. On the par-5 fifteenth, little Gene Sarazen holed a 225-yard four-wood for a double-eagle 2. Known ever since as golf's "shot heard round the world," that miraculous feat not only put Sarazen in a position to win the tournament the next day, but fired the imagination of the public.

In the post-war years, the advent of television brought the Masters into millions of American homes, and it quickly became an annual national tradition. It is the only major tournament that is held on the same course every year, but from the beginning of its association with television, Clifford Roberts set very strict ground rules for the broadcast, including the fact that only the back nine holes would be shown. This and many other quaint but charming old-world traditions surrounding the Masters have created a certain mystique, akin to some ancient and secret fraternity, surrounding the club and the tournament.

Syringomyelia
A Long, Painful Struggle

The condition that felled Bobby Jones was and is relatively rare, affecting only around two hundred thousand Americans currently. As the film depicts, Bobby suffered from a constellation of symptoms that varied in frequency and intensity, and it took quite a long time until these symptoms coalesced into a coherent diagnosis.

Syringomyelia is a neurological disorder in which a cavity forms in the spinal cord. The cavity, called a syrinx, fills with cerebrospinal fluid, and expands and elongates over time creating increasing pressure on the spinal cord. The cord is the main highway of the nervous system, connecting the brain to all parts of the body. As it becomes more severely damaged, the result can be pain, weakness, loss of sensation and muscle control, and eventually even paralysis. Some patients also experience impairment of internal organs and systems and other autonomic functions controlled by the nervous system.

Syringomyelia can be a congenital disorder, or it can arise as the result of some trauma, such as a serious fall or accident. The condition can remain dormant and undetected for years and years, and it is not uncommon that it is not recognized or identified until mid-life, as with Bobby Jones. The onset of pain in the extremities, and the slow loss of motor control that the film depicts as affecting Bobby are typical. These days, diagnosis and treatment have come a long way, particularly through the use of MRI (Magnetic Resonance Imaging). Surgical and other interventions are available that can alleviate the symptoms of syringomyelia, but if a diagnosis is made too late in the course of the disease, irreversible damage can occur.

It is estimated that about 210,000 Americans currently suffer from syringomyelia. To put those numbers in perspective, there are about three times as many Americans with cerebral palsy, four and a half million with Alzheimer's, and seventeen million with diabetes. The family of Bobby Jones has devoted a great deal of their time and attention to raising awareness about the disease, and to improving the lives of patients and their families. In the spring of 2004, just before the release of *Stroke of Genius*, the American Syringomyelia Alliance Project, a medical and patient support and awareness group, held a charity ball at which Robert Tyre Jones IV and Mimi Jones Hedwig, grandchildren of the great golfer, delivered keynote speeches.

For additional information, contact:

American Syringomyelia Alliance
Project, Inc.
P.O. Box 1586
Longview, TX 75606-1586
1-800-ASAP-282
www.asap.org

OPPOSITE: By the time he returned to St. Andrews in 1958, Bobby was already severely debilitated by his disease.

Giving Back

Bobby Jones' Greatest Legacy

It has become a source of great pride for golfers everywhere that their game has "given back" to local communities and residents an amazing amount of goodwill and charitable donations, to the benefit of countless people and organizations throughout the world.

Robert Tyre Jones, Jr. began his philanthropic efforts as a teenager by playing a series of exhibition matches during World War I for the benefit of the American Red Cross. Over his illustrious career and even into his retirement, Jones was dedicated to the goal of giving back whenever and wherever he could. Even when he was ill himself and could easily have begged off, Jones unselfishly led by example: playing in matches that would benefit individuals, friends, acquaintances, the PGA War Relief Fund, his beloved USGA, churches, schools, and countless children's groups.

One of his most notable quotes was: "A man never stands so tall as when he stoops to help a boy." It is this tradition that has given rise to an amazing array of philanthropy that is perhaps best manifested in the East Lake Community Foundation and the Charlie Yates Golf Course. These initiatives can be traced back to Jones himself.

While Jones grew up and played at East Lake Golf Club, time and circumstance took their toll on the venerable clubhouse and grounds as well as the surrounding neighborhood. By the early 1990s, the area of East Lake, Georgia, was in serious trouble. Invoking the giving spirit of Jones, a private family foundation and concerned citizens joined forces to create the East Lake Community Foundation. What has taken place in less than a decade is one of the most remarkable and inspirational community redevelopments ever.

Where drugs and crime once prevailed, families now engage in educational, cultural, and sporting lifestyles that serve as a model for communities everywhere. Where there was literally no hope for the future, there is now immense pride, personal and group achievement, and a sense that by working together people cannot only reach our goals, but can truly reach out and help others. New schools, stores, housing, community centers, and two wonderful golf courses adorn the East Lake community today.

Jones would certainly never have wanted the credit for such achievements; this was not his style. Nor is it the style of the generous folks who have made this

East Lake Community transformation possible. But all would agree that GOLF, though just a game, has been a remarkable catalyst of this and many other note-worthy examples of goodwill.

Around the United States and throughout the world, golf has accounted for more charitable giving than any other sport. At the professional level, The PGA TOUR is making a significant impact. The PGA TOUR last year alone donat-ed nearly $83 million to over 2,000 deserving groups. And children are at the center of attention through such efforts as The First Tee® (a World Golf Foundation initiative), a dynamic and powerful youth initiative that affords boys and girls around the world the opportunity to learn valuable life skills through the same game that Bob Jones began playing as a boy in 1908. It is impossible to calculate the enormous good that has come from these charitable efforts *because lifting the spirit and giving hope truly is priceless.*

What golf and men and women like Robert Tyre Jones, Jr. have done is set an example of what is good and gracious in our world. The game, played seriously, instills a sense of honor and integrity that can carry forward into all aspects of life.

The producers of *Stroke of Genius* determined from the outset that it would be important to pay tribute to Jones' giving spirit. To facilitate this, the producers worked to create "stakeholders" from communities across the country, especially engaging community leaders from the worlds of golf and charity. A stakeholder was deemed to be a person of influence who committed to the film's suc-cess through direct investment in it. These investments could be financial or philanthropic in nature, but motivated the stakeholder to be a vested champion for the film's success.

This stakeholder strategy reflects the approach that Bobby Jones himself adopted in launching epic undertakings like Augusta, the Masters, and a host of other remarkable initiatives during his lifetime. *He created groups of friends that willed projects to life.* This stakeholder strategy was consistently exe-cuted from the inception of the film venture. Concurrent with the founding of Bobby Jones Film, LLC, the producers created the Bobby Jones Film Foundation, a fund of the Private Consulting Group Foundation, under the direction of Film Foundation President Paul Brooks. The producers allocated a percentage of their film property receipts to charity, and the first checks issued out of the operating budget went to charities such as the East Lake Community Foundation and the Atlanta History Center. The film's investors also allocated several hundred thousand dollars of "seed funding" to the Film Foundation, in part to ensure the philanthropic legacy of this ambitious venture.

As the film moved toward production, the producers staged a six-city "Searching for Bobby Jones Audition Tour," sponsored by American Airlines, which engaged thousands of people in the excitement of auditioning for key roles in the film and learning more about Jones. We worked hard to be ambassadors of goodwill wherever we went.

As the promotion phase of the film began, the producers committed to an unprecedented strategy. A "Hometown Pre-Release Screening for Charity" at the Fox Theatre in Atlanta kicked off a grassroots, philanthropic tour across America, featuring a series of pre-release screenings for charity in top U.S. markets. A number of prestigious country clubs as well as a host of wonderful charitable organizations worked with the producers and a talented marketing team (led by Betsy Wiersma, Jim Malloy, and Julie Abels) to make these pre-release screenings memorable and to raise millions of dollars for charity.

In addition, private screenings were held at key gatherings including the PGA Merchandising Show, the National Conference for the Club Managers of America, and The First Tee's annual convention. This created tremendous grassroots "buzz" about the film that we could not afford to manufacture any other way, while concurrently advancing our philanthropic agenda.

As part of the ongoing philanthropic strategy for this film, the producers have teamed with the Helixx Group, PCG, and IMG to establish a national golf charity event called *The Bobby Jones Film National Day of Golf for Charity*. This legacy event, which has been seeded by a significant grant from the film's investors, will be held on the longest Monday of the year each year, beginning June 21, 2004. This event's unique format will be a fitting tribute to a man that many consider to be the pioneer of today's charitable golf movement.

All of this is an essential part of this film venture because—though the studios did not embrace the idea—this project is about more than just a movie. It is about a man and his legacy of goodwill. This is why we call the stakeholders of S*troke of Genius* "Legacy Partners of Robert Tyre Jones, Jr."

As O.B. Keeler, played by Malcolm McDowell in the movie, so eloquently says: "There are finer things in life than winning championships." Restoring hope, fulfilling dreams, and touching lives in a positive way are all part of the rich heritage of the game of golf. There are indeed "finer things," and in the world of golf, they can be attributed in no small part to the legacy given us by Mr. Jones, who truly raised the bar for those of us who would play behind him.

For more information on the mission and work of The Bobby Jones Film Foundation or The Bobby Jones Film National Day of Golf for Charity, please visit http://www. JonesFilmFoundation.org

A Miraculous Record

Over the years, the attention focused on Bobby Jones' successful completion of the "Grand Slam" of golf has somewhat overshadowed his stunning overall record of victories. Bobby's winning percentage is unequalled in golf, or in any other sport for that matter. In the "fat years" from 1923 to 1930, Bobby won 13 of the 21 national championships he entered. That's like a baseball player batting over .620 in championship games. In addition, he finished no worse than second in eleven of the last twelve open championships in which he played. No golfer, not Jack Nicklaus, not Arnold Palmer, not Tiger Woods, has been so dominant in tournament play. (By comparison, Jack Nicklaus, over a much, much longer career, has won 20 "majors" compared to Jones' 13, but 6 of those were Masters victories—a tournament that Bobby Jones founded after he had retired from competitive golf.) In much the same way pundits now talk about PGA events as "Tiger versus the field," Jones set the standard in his day. Despite the presence of such talented and wily champions as Walter Hagen and Gene Sarazen, it was always Jones who was the man to beat. In addition to the many individual crowns Bobby won, he also participated in five consecutive Walker Cup victories by the United States over Great Britain, every second year from 1922 to 1930.

Bobby Jones holds well over a dozen records in the U.S. Amateur Championship that still stand today, including most titles won, most times appearing as a finalist, and best winning percentage.

Even before Bobby won the Grand Slam, he was the first golfer to achieve what is called the "Double," that is, winning both the U.S. and British Open Championships in the same year, 1926. It was not until three years later that the Grand Slam became a realistic possibility. Bobby, of course, was neither gregarious nor boastful, so it's no surprise that he shared his grand scheme with no one, not even O.B. Keeler, but the fact is that as 1930 dawned, Jones had a plan clear in his mind: to win all four majors, which at that time meant both the Amateur and Open championships in both the United States and the United Kingdom. Later, when asked directly about it, he said, "I felt reluctant to admit that I considered myself capable of such an accomplishment…actually, I did make plans for that golfing year with precisely this end in view." At a loss for words to describe an achievement of such unprecedented magnitude, one sportswriter dubbed Bobby's four major victories the "impregnable quadrilateral of golf." And naturally, it was O.B. Keeler who first used the bridge term, "Grand Slam," to describe the feat. Keeler immortalized Bobby's actions: "This victory, the fourth major title in the same season and in the space of four months, had now and for all time entrenched Bobby Jones safely within the 'Impregnable Quadrilateral of Golf,' that granite fortress that he alone could take by escalade, and that others may attack in vain, forever." It should also be remembered that in his Grand Slam year, Bobby also played on the victorious U.S. Walker Cup team.

What makes Bobby's championship record even more remarkable is that even at the height of his playing career, he spent relatively little time on the golf course, whereas most of his competitors were pros. The joke was that Bobby played no more golf than the average doctor, which was in fact true.

Bobby Jones' Record in Majors

1916 U.S. AMATEUR – defeated in quarterfinals by Bob Gardner, Merion Cricket Club, Ardmore, PA.

1919 U.S. AMATEUR – defeated in finals by D. Davidson Herron, Oakmont, PA.

1920 U.S. AMATEUR – defeated in finals by Francis Ouimet, Engineer's Country Club, Roslyn, NY.
U.S. OPEN – tied for 8th place, Inverness Club, Toledo, OH.
BRITISH OPEN – withdrew during second round. Old Course, St. Andrews, Scotland.

1921 U.S. Amateur – defeated in quarterfinals by Willie Hunter, St. Louis Country Club, Missouri.
British Amateur – defeated in fourth round by Alan Graham, Royal Liverpool Golf Club, Hoylake, England.
U.S. Open – tied for 5th place, Columbia Country Club, Chevy Chase, MD.

1922 U.S. Amateur – defeated by Jess Sweetser in semi-final, The Country Club, Brookline, MA
U.S. Open – tied for 2nd place, Skokie, Country Club, Glencoe, IL.
Walker Cup – defeated Roger Wethered among others as US won at National Golf Links of America, Southampton, NY.

1923 U.S. Amateur – defeated in the second round by Max Marston, Flossmoor, Country Club, IL
U.S. Open – Won first Open tournament, Inwood Country Club, NY.

1924 U.S. Amateur – defeated George Von Elm in the final to win. Merion, Ardmore, PA.
U.S. Open – 2nd place, Oakland Hills Country Club, Birmingham, MI.
Walker Cup – lost doubles match but won singles on way to U.S. victory at Garden City Golf Club, Garden City, NY.

1925 U.S. Amateur – defeated Watts Gunn to win final, Oakmont Country Club, Oakmont, PA.
U.S. Open – 2nd place, Worcester Country Club, Worcester, MA.

1926 U.S. Amateur – defeated in the finals by George von Elm, Baltusrol Golf Club, Springfield, NJ.
British Amateur – defeated in the 6th round by Andrew Jamieson, Muirfield, Scotland
U.S. Open – Won at Scioto Golf Club, Columbus, OH.
British Open – Won at Royal Lytham and St. Annes, England
Walker Cup – Won all his matches in U.S. victory at St. Andrews, Scotland

1927 U.S. Amateur – defeated Chick Evans to win at Minikahada Club, Minneapolis, MN.
U.S. Open – tied for 11th place at Oakmont.
British Open – won at St. Andrews, Scotland

1928 U.S. Amateur – defeated T. Philip Perkins to win at Brae Burn Country Club, West Newton, MA.
U.S. Open – tied for 2nd place at Olympia Fields Golf Club, Matteson, IL.
Walker Cup – won all his matches in the U.S. victory at Chicago Golf Club, Wheaton, IL.

1929 U.S. Amateur – defeated in the 1st round by Johnny Goodman, Pebble Beach, CA.
U.S. Open – Won at Winged Foot Golf Club, Mamaroneck, NY.

1930 U.S. Amateur – defeated Eugene Homans to win at Merion, Ardmore, PA.
British Amateur – defeated Roger Wethered to win at the Old Course, St. Andrews, Scotland.
U.S. Open – won at Interlachen Golf Club, Minneapolis, MN.
British Open – won at Royal Liverpool Golf Club, Hoylake, England.
Walker Cup – won all his matches in U.S. victory at Royal St. Georges, Sandwich, England.

I could take out of my life everything except my experiences at St. Andrews and I would still have had a rich and full life.

There are two very important words in the English language that are very much mis-used and abused. They are "friend" and "friendship." When I say to a person, "I am your friend," I have said about the ultimate. When I say, "You are my friend," I am assuming too much, for it is a possibility that you do not want to accept my friendship. When I have said as much about you, and you have done so much for me, I think that when I say, "You are my friends," under these circumstances, I am, at the same time, affirming my affection and regard for you and expressing my complete faith in you and my trust in the sincerity of your friendship.

Therefore, when I say now to you, "Greetings, my friends at St. Andrews," I know I am not presuming because of what has passed between us.

I hope I have not been too sentimental on this theme of friendship, but it is one that is so important at this time. It is another element of the sensitivity that you people have—a wonderful, warm relationship. Friendship should be the great note of this world golf meeting, because not only people, but nations need friends. Let us hope that this meeting will sow seeds which will germinate and grow into important friendships among nations later on.

I just want to say to you that this is the finest thing that has ever happened to me. Whereas that little cup was first in my heart, now this occasion at St. Andrews will take first place always. I like to think about it this way that, now officially, I have the right to feel at home in St. Andrews as much as I, in fact, always have done.

—Excerpt from Bobby Jones' address upon receiving the
"Freedom of the Royal Burgh of St. Andrews" October, 1958

Photo of St. Andrews, 2003, courtesy of Linda Priddy

BOBBY JONES FILM LLC proudly presents
a LIFE^n PRODUCTION
in association with DEAN RIVER PRODUCTIONS

A ROWDY HERRINGTON Film

Starring

JIM CAVIEZEL   CLAIRE FORLANI   JEREMY NORTHAM

Bobby Jones
STROKE
of GENIUS

with CONNIE RAY, BRETT RICE, and
MALCOLM McDOWELL as O.B. Keeler

Casting by BEVERLY HOLLOWAY
Costume designer BEVERLY SAFIER
Production design BRUCE MILLER
Edited by PASQUALE BUBA

Music composed by JAMES HORNER
Director of photography TOM STERN

Co-executive producers GREG GALLOWAY,
JIM VAN EERDEN, TOM CROW
Executive producers DAVE ROSS, RICK ELDRIDGE
Producers TIM MOORE, JOHN SHEPHERD
Supervising producer RICK ELDRIDGE
Produced by KIM DAWSON

Story by ROWDY HERRINGTON and KIM DAWSON
Screenplay by ROWDY HERRINGTON
and TONY DEPAUL and BILL PRYOR

Directed by ROWDY HERRINGTON

Suggested Reading

Robert T. Jones, Jr., O.B. Keeler, *Down the Fairway: The Golf Life and Play of Robert T. Jones, Jr.*, Stroke of Genius Collector's Edition Series, British American Publishing, Latham, NY, 2004. Available online at www.bobbyjonesthemovie.com

Martin Davis, *The Greatest of Them All: The Legend of Bobby Jones*, The American Golfer, Inc., Greenwich, CT, 1996.

Catherine Lewis, et al., *Golf, The Masters, and the Legacy of Bobby Jones*, Triumph Publishing, 2000.

O.B. Keeler, *The Bobby Jones Story*, Triumph Books, Chicago, IL, 2003.

Robert Tyre Jones, *Bobby Jones on Golf*, Main Street Books, New York, 1992.

Tom Crow, *For the Love of the Game*, Stroke of Genius Collector's Edition Series, British American Publishing, Latham, NY, 2004. Available online at www.bobbyjonesthemovie.com

Sidney L. Matthew, *The Life and Times of Bobby Jones*, I.Q. Press, Tallahassee, FL, 1995.

Sidney L. Matthew, editor, *The Wit and Wisdom of Bobby Jones*. Clock Tower Press, Chelsea, MI, 2003.

Dick Miller, Triumphant Journey: *The Saga of Bobby Jones and the Grand Slam of Golf*. Taylor Publishing, 1994.

David Owen, *The Making of the Masters: Clifford Roberts, Augusta National, and Golf's Most Prestigious Tournament*. Simon & Schuster, New York, 1999.

Acknowledgments

The people of Bobby Jones Film, LLC, wish to thank Dianne Henk of British American Publishing, and her co-workers, for bringing this quite daunting publication to life. You demonstrated an enduring commitment to excellence and a spirit of graciousness all along the way. Marty Elgison, thanks for giving us your support.

To publisher Esther Margolis, designer Timothy Shaner, writer David Sobel, editors Keith Hollaman and Shannon Berning, and production specialists Frank DeMaio and Paul Sugarman at Newmarket Press—thanks for your artful writing and design ideas. Your reputation in the industry is well deserved. Thanks also to Pat Story, our wonderful publicist who supplied interviews and assisted with the photo selection; Sid Matthew and Cindy Thompson in his office for invaluable help with the historical photographs; Angelo Venturelli and Karen Vonada at Studiophoto for producing the digital photos so efficiently; Andrew Duncan for his help on the set designs; and Dr. Rand Jerris for serving as our USGA Research expert.

In Atlanta we shot at Jones' home course, the East Lake Golf Club (which hosts The PGA TOUR Championships), and at several other remarkable venues: the Atlanta Athletic Club—River Course, the Capital City Club at Brookhaven, the Druid Hills Country Club, and Chateau Elan's Woodlands and Legends courses. We are grateful for the grace showed to us by all, and hope we have done you proud.

Thanks to The PGA TOUR players that have supported this project along the way: Brad Faxon, Peter Jacobsen, Billy Andrade, David Frost, Ben Crenshaw, and a host of others. And to Payne Stewart, a special champion of this film before others caught the vision, and one who traveled a Journey in many ways like that of Jones himself.

Alan McGregor of the St. Andrews Links Trust and Peter Dawson of The Royal and Ancient Golf Club gave us the privilege of filming on hallowed ground. Steven Carter and his staff at The St. Andrews Bay Resort and Spa provided us with wonderful production headquarters as well as golf locations that filmed very well as a variety of UK courses in the 1920s. Kings Barnes and Camby House were invaluable locations in St. Andrews as well.

We want to specially acknowledge three of our sponsors that were with us from very early on: Bobby Jones Sportswear, American Airlines, and Pringle of Scotland. Wachovia Bank (Ken Thompson and Jim Leavelle) served as lead financial partners, with support from Jim Lewis and team at First Bank of the Tetons and the great folks at Jackson State Bank.

And to the couples Crow, Keys, Jaycox, Eden, and Johnston: You are reading this because you never gave up, and considered it worthwhile to stay the course. Thank you for your trust. Tom Cousins, John Imlay, Jim Singerling, Lee Hetrick, Peter Dawson, Don Panoz, and the family of Charlie Yates: whatever good comes of our humble efforts is a credit to the spirit of Bobby Jones that is reflected by people like you.

For more information or movie merchandise, please visit: www.bobbyjonesthemovie.com